'Don't change Nepal, let Nepal change you'

Life-enhancing experiences of a woman visiting

Nepal across three decades

Janet Jones

Dedications

I wish to dedicate this book to all the amazing people I met in Nepal who welcomed me into their hearts and their lives.

I also wish to dedicate it to my two children, Paul and Claire, both of whom have continued to make me proud to be called their mum.

Acknowledgements

Many people have encouraged and supported me in different ways during the process of writing this book. My special thanks go to Monica, Gav, Janice, Irene, Linda, Nigel, Kath and Topsy. I must acknowledge my husband, Rod, who has been supportive and very patient with me when asked on numerous occasions to help with a word or sentence when brain fog crept in, and for his enviable computer skills.

Lastly, I want to sincerely thank two exceptional women in Nepal who befriended me and made my experiences in their country so memorable. These are Jagan Gurung and Savitri Chhetri – my Nepali sisters and friends forever.

Cover by Design Wall

Namaste

Going to Nepal for the first time was an epiphany. Everything, and I mean everything, was so new, exciting, extraordinary and, for me, life changing. I wanted everyone I met to share my feelings about the country and the people. Indeed, how could they not? When I got back home, I know I must have become a 'Nepal bore', talking about my experiences at every opportunity. That was fine when relating them to my studies and work, after all I was doing a degree in Third World studies and then went onto lecture in third world issues, but my family and friends could only take so much before they switched off. This did not deter me from reflecting and reliving my time there, in my mind anyway. Several years ago, I started to give talks to various groups of people, such as the WI, Soroptimists and church groups on different topics related to my travels. I tried to make the material light-hearted, yet informative and the talks were received very well. I lost count of the number of times I was told to write a book about my experiences by members of the audience. However, time always eluded me.

I had been going to Nepal every year since 1994, that is until the Covid pandemic put paid to any long haul travelling. My last trip was in January 2020 when I eventually persuaded my husband to come with me for the first time. I never go to Nepal in January/February, and I don't know what made me choose to go then. But how fortuitous we did not go later because within a few weeks the World went into lock down and we would not have had that last journey.

The grip of the Covid pandemic coincided with my retirement from work. Being forced into semi-confinement seemed a perfect and 'no excuse' opportunity to write my book. I already was missing planning for my next trip and had not even envisaged that it would not happen the following year due to Covid. Indeed, could anyone have predicted that the pandemic would last for so long? Reliving my time in Nepal through writing this book was going to be the second-best way of being there.

I have thoroughly enjoyed going down memory lane. One reminiscence triggered yet another. Whilst I have tried to produce some form of structure by writing in themed chapters, this is very loose. The first couple of chapters are giving the background of why I went to Nepal in the first place and why I continue to go back. My first impressions of travelling alone and arriving in the country are revealed and shows how new I was to this travelling lark. The next few chapters give a very personal account of a collection of some of my experiences. These are the more light-hearted ones, of getting around Nepal, rhino hunting, health and money matters, and communication difficulties. My interaction with beings in the natural world, from monkeys to rats to leeches, was particularly pertinent to me. What I was not expecting by putting pen to paper, or fingers to computer keys, was how therapeutic it became. I had not really realised how travelling on my own and all the encounters that brings had had such a profound effect on me, as a person. I suppose that is what is meant by 'discovering yourself'. The final chapter alludes to this and brings together how Nepal has changed me.

I do hope that you enjoy reading this book. Some of you will be reading it because you would like to compare it to your own travels to a developing country, some may have even been to Nepal. There are other people who will read this who will wish they could have a taste of travelling but think that travelling is for someone else to do, not them. That was me 28 years ago. My story, I hope, may inspire you to pack a rucksack and do the same as me.

Why Go to Nepal?

One of the most common questions asked of me is 'Why did you go to Nepal in the first place?' Sometimes, when I am struggling to cope with the terrain or the climate, I say that to myself. But I cannot imagine what my life would have been like had I not embarked on that first visit back in 1994. So, to answer the question, I will try to tell you why I got involved in Nepal, in a nutshell. I am not known for my conciseness, so please bear with me.

After spending the whole of my adult life, from when I married at the age of 18 years old, being a wife and mother, in 1992 my life changed beyond recognition. I had had a son, Paul, soon after we married and our daughter, Claire arrived three years later. She became extremely ill at 15 months with severe arthritis, which resulted in her suffering life-long constant pain, illness, and disability.

The following years were spent caring for Claire and trying to give both children as normal a life as possible. I did not resent this for one minute, but as the years went by, I felt that I wanted to do other things as well. I worked in shops part-time to fit around Claire's schooling and medical appointments and became heavily involved with several voluntary organisations relating to children in hospital, disability, and arthritis. I really enjoyed doing this as it was making something positive out of a negative situation. It also gave me a social life. Some of the work involved organising fund raising events. I always involved Claire and she became quite proficient at extracting money off people, by selling tickets for fashion shows or discos, or shaking a tin on flag days. Due to her medical condition and medication, Claire's growth had been stunted and so reached only 4'1" in her adulthood. I had always told her to make the best of what she had, and she certainly did that. A bit of moral blackmail and a cheeky grin worked wonders! Oh dear, did that make me a bad mother?

In 1992, I was walking in the park with my two dogs. One was a Labrador cross called Henge, who had been my son's dog. He had become a punk, Paul not the dog, and lots of punks had little black dogs. After a couple of years Henge did not fit into his wayward lifestyle and so we adopted him. The other dog was a Cavalier King Charles spaniel, Guy, who was my daughter's dog. She had many episodes of when she could not walk, so her dad or I took him for his walks. I had a 'light-bulb' moment as I was talking to some of my dog-walking friends. Now, I am used to being called 'Rod's wife', and 'Paul and Claire's mum' but I drew a line through being called 'Henge and Guy's grandma'. I knew, at that point, that something drastic had to change in my existence.

The year before, I had been to night classes to study for a GCSE in Sociology. I really enjoyed learning, which was totally opposite to my attitude at school many years before. I passed and asked the teacher if it was possible to do an A 'level. He suggested I enrol onto an Access course, which was a programme for people who wanted to continue in higher education but did not have the qualifications to do so. So, after my light-bulb moment, I enrolled on an Access course at my local university.

My only objective for doing the course was to carry on learning, nothing more. It was taught on two days a week for about nine months. It was a nightmare to arrange for people to pop in to check on Claire, but where there is a will there is a way. I loved it. I was suddenly 'Janet', belonging to no-one. I also found that I did have a brain. After more than twenty years of domesticity and focusing on just my family and what was going on immediately around me, I thought that any opinions I had were worthless. But the interaction with other people in the same boat as me, opened a whole new world. A few weeks after starting the course we were given a PCAS form to apply to do a degree. That totally freaked me out. I was not degree material. I was always led to believe that to go to university to do a degree you had to be rich, posh, or very clever. I was none of those. However, after studying the prospectus for the university I decided to apply because I wouldn't get in anyway.

I have a terrible affliction. It is called being a Libran. I cannot decide on anything, I sit on the fence in arguments, I hate conflict and injustice. True to my birth sign, I wanted to study all the courses in the prospectus. However, I settled on a new programme called 'Third World Development'. It appealed to me, not because I wanted to save the world, but it covered a lot of different subjects, such as economics, health, industrialisation, religion, sociology, gender, tourism, and introduced the concept of development and underdevelopment. Well, I did pass my Access exams and was given a place on the degree, and there were no fees. I was so lucky, as I did it when all citizens of the UK were awarded three years higher-level education. I would never have been able to pay for it otherwise.

The university was close to where I lived and so I was able to be 'on call' if needs be at home. Claire was nearly

6

20 years old by then and wanting more independence. I knew that as her main carer I would find it difficult to loosen the 'strings' if I was to have sat at home, so that was another reason for my decision to go to university, or at least to occupy my mind. She was also going through a reasonably steady phase in her condition and was working in a children's nursery. The use of an electric wheelchair was making her life easier.

University life was totally different from what I had imagined. Everyone was normal, with normal clothes and had normal conversations. I expected it to be terribly posh with long haired students wearing college scarves and having intellectual conversations in huddles. I don't think I have ever seen anyone in a scarf and certainly have never heard an intellectual conversation around the campus. I had been watching too much 'University Challenge'.

Anyway, now I am getting closer to the direct reason why I went to Nepal. So, hang in there. During my first week at uni, that's what us students call it, I had two modules of direct significance. One was 'Introduction to the Third World' and the other was 'Tourism in the Developing World'. The former module was fascinating. At my age of 42 years, I was aware of global inequalities, but to see it in statistics and specifics really brought it home to me. We were asked to produce a portfolio of any aspect in any country of the Third World. Oh dear, a Libran's nightmare – a free choice of country and topic. Where would I start? Luckily at the same time, for the other module, we were asked to produce another portfolio on tourism in a given country. I was given Nepal. My friend was given the Bahamas. I was envious because I did not even know where Nepal was. However, thinking I was saving time, I decided to do my first portfolio on social aspects of Nepal so that I could double up on research time for the tourism one. It also saved me from hours, if not days, of decision-making.

I really enjoyed the research and became enthralled in the country. Nepal seemed such a diverse place with regards to terrain, language, people, religion, in fact everything. It was also a popular tourist destination. I spent hours and hours searching the library for information, this was before internet times. During my research I constantly came across an organisation called the Annapurna Conservation Area Project (ACAP). It was a Nepali project addressing development in the Annapurna region of the Himalayas, focusing on social, environmental and tourism aspects. I really admired what they were doing and the fact that it was an indigenous project. It also had a strong emphasis on the involvement of women in the development process.

One day, near to the end of the first year at uni, I was sitting with some of the young students on my course and they were talking about what they were going to do in the summer. Several of them said that they were going overseas to travel or work. I was so envious. I had always wanted to travel but it hadn't been possible for lots of reasons. I sat there thinking, "I wish I could go somewhere like these young uns". Then I thought "Why not? OK, I had Claire to consider, I didn't have a passport, I had never flown, I hadn't travelled on my own before, I didn't have the money. But if I don't do it now, I never will". The ACAP project in Nepal jumped at me. I would love to go and work for a couple of weeks for them in the Himalayas. Yes, me! I was doing a degree in Third World Development and yet I had never been to a Third World country. Going to Nepal would surely help my studies.

I couldn't get the idea out of my head. I talked it over with my husband who thought I was mad, but eventually came round to my way of thinking, although I am sure that he thought I would not go through with the trip. I also talked it over with Paul and Claire, who said I should go for it. I contacted ACAP asking if I could do some voluntary work for them in Nepal and was then asked for my CV. It was the first time that I had done my CV and hadn't realised how much I had done over the years, with voluntary work, shop work, and so on. Eventually I heard back from them to say, "Yes come and work for us". I was to work in a village in the Himalayas called Ghandruk. I was over the moon and absolutely freaked out. What had I done? I must be mad. Wow!

Departure day was in about seven weeks. There was so much to do. I had to get a passport. I had to have my inoculations. There were a lot of them, including my childhood ones that I had avoided when I was at school. Remarkably, I did not faint. I had to book a flight, which seemed unreal booking one to 'Kathmandu'. Importantly, I had to get some money. I took out a £1000 student loan. We were allowed to do that then if it was to help with studying. And I needed to get my gear, including sturdy walking boots. I was not a big walker so had not possessed such items.

The local newspaper had got hold of my story for some strange reason and did a feature on me along with a photograph of me in a trekking pose in my front garden. It was very unrealistic as the background was not mountains and hills but semi-detached houses and parked cars. I was due to become a grandmother in the September so that was brought into the heading, 'Allestree grandmother blazing a trail for tourists.' Embarrassing or what! During the trip, the reporter phoned Claire for updates on my adventure. She obviously did not know what I was doing, as the updates were very short.

A couple of weeks before departing I was put in touch with two people who had been to the village of Ghandruk and had worked for ACAP. One was a girl who had worked for the organisation for a few weeks. She enjoyed her time there, but it was particularly challenging, especially as she had to sleep in a cow shed with the buffalo.

The other person was an elderly man who visited the area frequently. He told me that it was a long hard walk to the village, which could last for three days if the road was blocked. He also said that there was a typhoid outbreak in the village at the moment. He asked me if I was ready for the culture shock? I replied that I was as I had been brought up in Leek. I don't think he understood my humour. Both conversations made me question my sanity, yet at the same time, made me even more excited. I couldn't relate any of those possible experiences to anything I had done before or even envisaged. That was what I wanted, wasn't it? My adventure was starting. I would never be the same again.

Another question asked by and of me is 'Why do you keep going back to Nepal?' The simple answer is that I love the country. However, I must admit that as I am driven to the airport to go back home, I always say to myself that I will not be coming back. Kathmandu, in particular, is dirty and smelly with pollution, some of the people drive me crazy, and I've seen everything what I want to see there. Then, as I get into the air on the plane, plans for my next trip to Nepal pop into my head. It is like a drug that draws you back into its addiction. It is said that once you have been to Nepal you will want to go again. Most people find that is true.

My first trip there was a 'one-off' or so I expected. I worked in a children's nursery in Ghandruk, which was amazing and a tremendous eye-opener. I caught the bug, literally, but also the travelling bug. The next year I went back to research for my independent study for my degree. I had an incredible time interviewing local women on their role in women's development, followed by a visit the following year to say thank you to the women who had been interviewed and to say my good-byes. I had photographed each of the women and on this trip brought them a copy in a frame as a 'thank you' gift. One of the women from the low caste community had her photo taken while she was breast feeding her baby boy. When I went back, the baby had died, and the photograph was the only one she had had of her son. We hugged each other as we both cried. I was getting more and more attached to Nepal.

As my degree was coming to an end, I had to decide what was next. I really enjoyed learning and particularly researching, and I wanted to justify going back to Nepal. The staff in my department at uni encouraged me to do a PhD. They could be very persuasive and, to cut a long story short, I agreed with them. I settled on looking into social aspects of leprosy in Nepal. It was something I was interested in, for lots of reasons. I had been to a church school and so listened and read the bible, feeling sorry for people with leprosy who were ostracised. It was also a potentially deforming condition, which I related to Claire's arthritis that could, and in some parts of her body were, deforming, yet she was treated in a very inclusive way whereas people affected by leprosy were not. I also witnessed harrowing sights of people affected by leprosy begging on the streets in Kathmandu and on the TV. My Libran tendencies made me want to investigate the cruelty of such a disease.

I knew little about leprosy, so I went to Nepal on a reconnaissance trip to build up some contacts, to meet people with leprosy, and to learn about the disease. I was fortunate to be directed to a leprosy shelter in Kathmandu where I met a doctor and physiotherapist who taught me the basics about the disease. It was there where I met many people affected by the disease for the first time. This was an amazing experience, and I heard many personal stories which confirmed that this was definitely the research I wanted to do. The shelter became the focus for my research. Over the next few years, I met and interviewed over 150 people affected by leprosy. I heard tales of dreadful discrimination and such courage. I travelled extensively throughout Nepal and interviewed people in lots of different settings, such as homes, hospitals, leprosy villages. I was so humbled and felt so privileged to be able to do the research.

I was only able to go out to Nepal for short bursts once a year, for two to three weeks at a time. My daughter was my top priority and was going through many difficult times with her disease. It was also only possible for me to visit Nepal for so many years as I did it on a shoestring and monsoon time is by far the cheapest season for flights and accommodation. I left it as late as possible, August/September so that I was not caught in the peak monsoon. I had also been asked to do some teaching at uni, so had to be back before the semester started. It is surprising how much research I could fit in in a short space of time.

Inevitably, as many people will know who have spent time in a country like Nepal, you can quickly get immersed into people's lives and causes. Nepal is a place whereby you are easily made to feel part of the society. Nepalese people are so generous with their time and hospitality, and it is not long before you are inundated with invitations to visit the receptionist/shop keeper/restaurant owner's home for a meal and to meet the family. I made some long-lasting friends during the years I have been there.

I have also become caught up in various 'causes', one such cause being an orphanage for jail children. In many developing countries, if a mother/father is imprisoned and has no one to look after their children, the children have to also stay in the prison, sharing their parent's space and rations. I had visited the male and female prison. The male prison, in particular, was not a pleasant environment for anyone, especially children. I saw evidence of physical and emotional abuse of more than one child. The orphanage was an extremely worthwhile cause as it looked after the children and gave them a stable and safe environment away from the prison. However, I had to withdraw from my involvement when the owner was accused of selling babies to help with the funding of the orphanage. But that is another story in itself.

Once my PhD was finished there was no way whatsoever that I could stop going back to Nepal. I continued to go back to visit friends. Unfortunately, in 2008 my daughter passed away. Her condition had been deteriorating and she had had to have her leg amputated. I had vowed that I would not leave her again, but the worst happened, and she died. Needless to say, I was devastated.

During my previous visit to Nepal, I had bought some silver jewellery and beads. Claire and I had decided to set up a small business, selling jewellery. Claire would have been able to manage that because it was small, light and could be easily transported. She was a bit of an entrepreneur so enjoyed the two sales that we managed before her death. I decided to carry on with the business in her name.

I also decided to set up a 'Claire Jones Memorial Fund' to raise funds for projects in Nepal. A large percentage of goods sold from the business was to go into the fund. I also did some fundraising through car boot sales, an annual garden fete, and gave talks to groups on Nepal. Whilst not raising large amounts of money, her fund provided three scholarships for children with disabilities to attend Ghandruk High school. Claire also worked as a nursery nurse, so it seemed appropriate to support the nursery in Ghandruk. It also contributed to other projects relating to disability, children, and women, such as, bricks to build a women's community room, drinking water provision in a village just outside Ghandruk, funds towards a water purifying machine to enable women to sell safe water to tourists to prevent the use of plastic bottles and to enable

14

income generation for the community, and education of other children. One of the latest projects was to provide a small rotavator for the women to till the soil. Most men had left Ghandruk to find work and the farming had been left to the women. I know Claire would have approved. That was important to me. Consequently, each year that I go back I check on the projects that 'Claire's' money goes to and to buy some goods for my business. I have drifted from jewellery to bags and purses made from ethical sources. I really hate shopping, but it is different in Nepal. I am not given a cup of tea when I go to Sainsbury's in Derby.

You will gather by now that my annual visits to Nepal are as a result of my love for the country and its people along with my desire to make something good out of, in my opinion, the tragedy of my daughter's death. A few years ago, I started to write a book on 'ordinary' women in Nepal. I have interviewed women who would not hit the headlines with their stories but, as a Westerner, find their lives incredibly interesting. To me, it is impossible to not be fascinated by the 'ordinary' stories of a woman having to listen while her son was murdered by the Maoists; the life of a female Maoist soldier; a woman given away at five days old because the village lama (Buddhist spiritual leader) had predicted that if she stayed in her family home her father would die; or witnessing a jhakri (traditional medical practitioner) using her healing ability derived from two white snakes that live inside her body. The book is a long process, but I continue to collect more stories from these remarkable women.

I have tried to answer the two questions that I am often asked, in a nutshell. I warned you that I am not renowned for my conciseness. But there were no quick answers to why I went to Nepal in the first place and why I keep going. Many people do not understand my fascination for Nepal, but they have not been there. I hope that you enjoy my stories of some of the more light-hearted true experiences that I have had and come to your own conclusion as to whether I am deluded or not. I am sure that many people reading this will have faced similar experiences. I am not saying I am any better or braver than anyone else. Some people may even think that I am a wuss. I often do. However, I do know that by reflecting on my time in Nepal has made me realise that I will never take for granted the opportunities I have been given in my life; to have my children, go onto higher education and to visit this beautiful country.

First impressions

On July 21st 1994, I set off for the airport to embark on the journey that would change my life for ever. There I was, at the age of 43 years, loading into the boot of the car a 20kg rucksack rammed full of clothes and strange things that I might need, 'just in case', such as, string, pegs, bath plugs in different sizes, mossi spray, Mosquito net, antihistamine spray and cream, water purifying tablets, rape alarm, candles, first aid kit, penknife, toilet roll, pillowcase. I was flying from Gatwick, which was a long way from home, but my husband had offered to drive me down there as he could visit his parents who lived near to the airport.

As we drove down the M1 my mind was full of advice people had given to me during the weeks leading up to departure day: "Don't drink the water". "Only drink bottled water". "Peel your fruit". "Don't eat salads". "Don't have ice in your drinks". "Pace yourself". "Wash your hands often". "Keep your arms and legs covered, especially at night, because of mosquitoes". "Watch out for spiders". "Hide your money". "Watch your purse". "Be careful in crowds". "Don't walk about after dark". "Keep your wedding ring on". "Lock your bedroom door". "Put a chair against your bedroom door". "You must be mad". "Don't go". I took on board the well-meaning guidance, yet tried to block out the attached negativity, to concentrate on my positive thoughts of experiencing another culture, language, food, travel, and lifestyle.

I must admit that I was quite nervous, yet excited. As I have said in the introduction, it will be the first time I have flown; the first time I have had a passport, and the first time I have been anywhere on my own. I also felt extremely guilty about leaving my daughter behind. My husband would be around most of the time and I had some excellent and supportive friends who would step in if needs be. What is more, she was going through a 'good phase', which was great for her, and she was able to walk, which was always a bonus. She also gave me her blessing to go. My son started to introduce me to his mates as his 'get on down mother', which I took as an approval of my trip.

Rod dropped me off at the airport and suddenly I was on my own. Now the adventure really starts. I flew by Royal Nepal Airlines, which was the flagship of Nepal. We were all greeted onto the plane by Nepali female cabin crew beautifully dressed in pink and blue saris, who held their hands together in front of their faces and said "Namaste". Namaste means 'hello' and 'welcome' in Nepali and is a word that I will be hearing and using time and time again over my next 26 years.

I must admit that as the plane door was shut, I had a little panic moment, but it soon passed. There was no turning back. We had two stops on the way, one in Frankfurt to have the plane cleaned, and one in Dubai. I was really having an adventure, I thought. These interludes gave me the opportunity to see who else was going to Kathmandu. People from all over the world were getting on the plane. I suppose that I had quite a sheltered life with regards to mixing with people who were not British or White, except for my own mother who came from Germany. I was always fascinated by different cultures, and so the mix of nationalities I saw was so interesting and added to my excitement. I also was reassured to see many women, either on their own or with small groups of other women. I had been made to feel that I was doing something extraordinary and risky by venturing to Asia on my own. Seeing these women, I felt that I was one of many womenfolk looking for a different lifestyle, even if for a short period. It was an empowering feeling.

The flight was long but, as it was my first flight, I found it interesting. I watched a film, Mr Bean'. I am not usually into Mr Bean or Rowan Atkinson, but I really enjoyed it, especially as everyone seemed to be laughing, regardless of nationality. It was one of those films which had minimal dialogue and so language was not a barrier.

There were also lots of meals and snacks brought around. I did find it strange to be offered alcoholic drinks with my breakfast. I usually have milk on my cornflakes. The flight seemed to go without a hitch, although there was little leg room. I wasn't able to sleep as I usually like the foetal position, which was out of the question. I was fascinated by the cloud formations under our aeroplane. And, when it was possible to see the land below, I would try and work out what we would fall on if the plane crashed. I tried to put those kinds of thoughts out of my mind as they were not healthy. I hadn't realised how much sand there was in the world. It seemed to go on and on for hours. At least it would be a soft landing if the worst was to happen.

I had been told that if I look out of the plane window, on the left, as we approach Nepal, we could have a stunning view of the Himalayas. Unfortunately, as it was monsoon time, the mountains were covered in cloud, and so I didn't see them or anything else until we were coming down towards Kathmandu and we dropped through the clouds. My first view was of the foothills. They were lush and green, and much was terraced. There were tiny houses perched on top of some of the hills and on the sides. I wondered how people got to them as there did not appear to be any roads. I could just make out some rivers that looked like grey lines from where I was sitting.

Suddenly, we were over the Kathmandu Valley, which was surrounded by the hills. The land was much flatter and by then we were nearer to the ground. Lots of small settlements were spotted, either by the river or a road. Then, a huge mass of buildings materialised. This was Kathmandu, my first glimpse. There were lots of roads but there did not seem to be much traffic. The buildings were quite tightly packed, many seemed to be unfinished, with only the first or second floor completed. Strange! I could see a big white building which was the King's palace, I was told, and I could make out several pagoda type temples dotted among the streets. There was a break in the density of the buildings and then another large settlement, which I was told was Patan.

By the time we landed in Kathmandu I was aching and tired but so excited that I was buzzing. I am here. I have done it! It was raining as we disembarked, but it didn't dampen my mood. Everywhere was so calm and all the ground staff were so smiley. We had to go through passport control. I got in the queue that said 'Foreigners with visas', which was slow, but it did give me time to look around the big hall. It was very ornate, with wooden screens and pillars beautifully carved with animals or gods. The walls were embellished with giant posters of activities and places in Nepal. Everywhere looked so inviting.

The baggage claim was quite the opposite. There was just one carousel for the baggage. The walls were a dingy grey and everywhere looked shabby. It was a place where you didn't want to hang around too long. The bags had not been unloaded from the plane yet, so I decided to go to the toilet. I was prepared for a squat latrine, although not for the lack of hygiene. I will leave that to your imagination. What I was not prepared for was the unbearable stench of urine and ammonia that hit me even before I reached the toilets. After that visit, I became quite proficient at holding my breath during the whole toilet process. This would keep me in good stead for any future visits to public toilets.

I went back to the baggage carousel to find my rucksack. Unfortunately, I had not taken into consideration that, as Nepal was a major trekking destination, many other people had rucksacks. I watched them go around and around, peering intently at each one to see if it was mine. I had loaned the rucksack off a friend, and I couldn't remember what it looked like. Indeed, they all looked remarkably similar. I waited for all the other passengers to claim theirs until there was only a handful left on the carousel. At last, I spotted mine. It was green and red. I must remember that for future use. I was sorted. A nice porter got me a trolley and even pushed it through the customs corridor and out of the building. I hadn't realised that I had to 'tip' him. I had no Nepali money on me, so I gave him some English change. He seemed happy with that.

Up until now, everything was remarkably calm and organised. I wondered what all the fuss was about. This travelling lark was a doddle. However, as I left the building, I was hit by total chaos. Just outside were dozens of men all shouting. "Do you need a taxi?" "I know a good hotel". "Let me take your bag." I froze. I was to be met by someone from the organisation I was to be volunteering for. I didn't know if it was a man or woman, let alone the name. Suddenly, I heard my name being called. I scanned the throng and there was a Nepali man holding up a brown envelope and on it written in yellow "Janet Jones". I was so relieved. I pushed my way through the jostling crowd and met my rescuer. He told me to follow him, and we went to a 4x4 in the car park.

Once installed in the car, we set off from the airport to where I would be staying. The airport grounds that we had to drive through were very neat and were laid out with nice bushes, trees, and flowers. I started to feel relaxed again and sank back into the security of the leather seats. So far, so good.

However, within seconds we were driving along the ring road. Wow, it was unbelievable. There were hundreds of people at the side of the road or on the road. Some were just walking, but others were trading. There were women sitting by small fire braziers roasting corn or other delicacies. Men were playing some sort of dice game. Children were playing in the piles of rubbish at the side of the road, alongside dogs and cows. They were not wearing shoes, which made me wince with the thought of what they might stand on. The traffic was unbelievable. By the time we came out of the airport it was peak traffic time. I have been in 'traffic jams' at home but this was something else. Not only were there cars, buses, lorries, tuk tuks and motor bikes, some with a whole family riding pillion, but buffalo, and people trying to weave in and out of the vehicles. There did not seem to be any traffic regulations. Vehicles used any lane and just headed forward, being successful if they could hold their nerve before the on-coming vehicle moved out of the way.

The noise of people and traffic was something you only hear on the television when showing clips of Delhi or other overcrowded cities. There were sounds from pedestrians shouting, and traders calling out. The vehicles were peeping to make others to move out of the way, which was impossible. The vehicle horns were not just ordinary 'beep, beep'. Oh no, they were Christmas songs, and even 'He's a jolly good fellow'.

The smells hit my nostrils as we drove on. There were traffic fumes, of course, smoke, food cooking, rotting food, latrine odours, incense and perfume that tried to disguise the, not so pleasant, odours. The pollution hit me the most. The traffic fumes struck me at the back of my throat and stayed with me for the remainder of my visit. My skin felt very sweaty and clammy with the humidity. I was stuck to my seat; my hands were sticky, and sweat was pouring off my face and into my eyes. What a sight I must have been! I turned to my right, and I thought that I was imagining what I saw. A monkey. A live monkey just sitting on a high wall. I heard that they had monkeys in Nepal, but never imagined that they would be in an urban setting, amidst all the people and traffic.

We had only driven half a mile and I was in absolute shock. My mind was having trouble taking this all in and I had my chin on my chest in awe. All this time my fellow

23

passenger was talking to me. He was actually a senior member of the organisation that I was going to be attached to and was trying to hold an intelligent conversation with me. But I was speechless and could mumble only a few coherent words. Fortunately, we had many conversations since then, so I was able to show him that I was not a total gibbering idiot.

The traffic and people thinned out after a while which gave me the chance to pull myself together and to take in the surroundings. The 'half-built' structures that I had seen from the plane were residential and commercial properties, that were occupied. Many had steel rods poking out of the top for when they want to carry on building another floor. Forward thinking, I guessed. Most of the shops were small but crammed full of everyday produce. There were workshops in action, building furniture, mending bicycles, or welding mechanical bits and pieces. All the buildings were constructed so that their frontages were close to the road. It was, therefore, easy to see the shopkeepers sitting in the doorway, their children playing on the narrow pathway. I noticed that some shops even had beds inside. I was told later that many shops are used by the whole family as homes, as well. Everything was a real eye-opener. I suppose that the journey was an introduction to my first of many culture shocks.

After about 30 minutes of travelling, we drove into Thamel. Thamel is the tourist area, where most of the shops, budget hotels and entertainment were found. The roads were very narrow and bumpy. It looked to be a vibrant area, with shops upon shops of jewellery, trekking gear, carpets, clothes, felt goods, shawls, antique artifacts, bags and anything else you could imagine. Much of the merchandise was hanging outside on wires or on telegraph posts or even on religious shrines. My eyes darted from one side of the road to the other trying to absorb everything they could see. I tried to make a mental note of where I had seen something I liked but gave up.

Because it was monsoon season, there were not too many tourists around, so the atmosphere was quite subdued, but my excitement was building up again. I wondered if my companion could hear my heart thumping. Suddenly we came to a stop. We had turned into a short driveway in the middle of what looked like the central road in Thamel. We were saluted by a smart, uniformed man. We had arrived at my destination, the notable Kathmandu Guest House.

As I got out of the car and looked around, I had a feeling that this is what being in colonial India would have been like. It was an oasis in the middle of an urban desert. The building was an old Rana palace that had been converted into the first and most known hotel in Kathmandu. Much of the older building was ornately carved, as in the airport, in dark wood, although, an unattractive 60s' type extension had been built on the side to accommodate more guests. The courtyard at the front was bedecked with tables and chairs which were protected from the elements by large umbrellas. There were several people having refreshments at the tables, being served by male waiters dressed in traditional Nepali costume, of black trousers, white shirts, grey apron, and a topi hat. There was a beautiful smell of jasmine and traditional Nepali music was being quietly played in the background. The ambience of the place oozed safety and peace, a direct contrast to the mayhem of the journey from the airport. I liked it, I really liked it, thank goodness.

My companion bade me farewell and there I was alone in a foreign country. It was late afternoon by now and I checked into my room. The reception and my room were covered in beautiful wooden carvings and the ceilings were painted with bright flowers. I had a bathroom to myself, and the bed looked and felt wonderfully comfortable. This was real luxury in comparison to what I was expecting. I had a lovely view onto the back garden, with a pristine lawn and small shrine to one of the gods at one end. I was paying more than I could afford but the organisation who I would be working for had put me here. On reflection I suppose it was a good idea to stay somewhere like this on my first visit to a developing country. For a while, it protected me from the harsh realities of Nepal.

I realised that I had not had anything to eat for several hours and so decided to check out the food at the hotel. But before that, I thought I would just pop my head out of the hotel drive and onto the street. It seemed quite busy by then as tourists were making their way to the various restaurants for food. I was approached by a man asking if I wanted to book a hang-glide or white-water rafting. I declined as I did when I was offered a full body massage by someone else. Another man approached me to buy some Tiger Balm. A beggar arrived asking for money. I did not know what to say. A tuk tuk stopped and offered to take me on a trip around Kathmandu. I was overwhelmed and quite disturbed by all the attention I had attracted. Is this what it is going to be like all the time? Would I cope? What was I doing here?

I went back into the safety of Kathmandu Guest House and sat at one of tables. I was really thirsty due to the humidity. I didn't know what to order to quench my thirst. The waiter suggested San Miguel and I agreed because I did not want to disagree with him. He brought me a litre bottle of the beer and I ordered a meal, a vegetable lasagne. I really should have ordered water, but I couldn't see it on the menu. I was too embarrassed to ask for it. What a wuss! I didn't even drink alcohol, but I was so thirsty I drank it all during the meal. It went down well.

That night I was so tired after my long journey. It was more than twenty-four hours from when I left home to arriving in Kathmandu. I couldn't wait to get into my bed and was sure to sleep like a log. I lay there expecting sleep to take over me. But no, I couldn't sleep. I had had so much mental stimulation since my arrival, and it was going around and around in my head. All the sights, sounds, smells, even the feel of the city, came flooding into my mind. I was not horrified or disappointed or put off the trip, but totally overwhelmed in a really exciting way. And this was only day one.

I reflected on my experience earlier when I left the sanctuary of the hotel. Yes, I had been unnerved and somewhat frightened. But hadn't that been why I had come to a country like Nepal, to experience different cultures and to prove to myself that I was capable of existing out of my comfort zone? If I was going to be frightened of being approached and trying new things, then I might as well stay in my hotel room for the duration of my visit or go home. At that point, I made a pact with myself that I would not let anything I was exposed to frighten me enough to stop me from experiencing Nepal. Perhaps I was being a bit rash, but I felt so privileged to be here and to be given opportunities that I could only dream of before, that nothing was going to stop me, especially me. My goodness, what will the rest of the visit have in store for me now? My adventure was really under way, and I was going to make the very most of it.

Getting around and about

Taking journeys, no matter how long or short, around Nepal can be very testing on your nerves, physical stamina, and sanity. Some of the roads in the cities are now 'reasonable', meaning they do not have immense potholes and are made of concrete, not mud. Those roads in my early years were downright dangerous. The smaller and side roads are still suicidal, with large potholes or mounds of rubble in the centre. Many are dissected with drainage work. There are no florescent barriers to warn pedestrians or drivers of their condition. Travelling at night is taking your life in your hands, as there are few streetlights to show drivers or pedestrians the way. During the monsoon, the roads are even more treacherous, as the holes fill with rain and their condition is compounded by blocked drains. I went into a shop in Kathmandu one afternoon during the rains, and when I came out the road was knee deep in water. The urban roads, particularly in the old parts of Kathmandu, are so narrow, with vehicles, particularly motor bikes, parked haphazardly, it is a miracle that any cars can get through them without being damaged.

The rural roads are another thing. The main roads, during the dry season, are 'reasonable' but they degenerate into broken lumps of concrete, often blocked with landslides in the monsoon season. Many of the roads are classed as 'off-road' meaning they are just tracks but are used by buses and cars. These are the 'roads' that go to the smaller villages or into the foothills. The surfaces are mainly mud or sometimes, gravel. It is not uncommon to encounter lorries or buses that are mud-bound and have been for several hours. It is then all hands-on deck to get them out. Most of these roads are also graced with deep drops of several hundred feet on one side, just to add to the 'interest' of any journey.

The first few years I only travelled around Kathmandu and the valley, and to Pokhara and Ghandruk. When I was conducting research for my PhD, I went much further afield to places such as Janakpur and Nepalgunj in the very south of Nepal, and Birendranagar, a town in the Mid-West of Nepal. These locations are remote, even by Nepali standards. When I say 'remote' I mean that they can only be reached by plane or several days walk from the nearest town, or by an exceptionally long drive from Kathmandu or Pokhara.

One of my first research trips was to Birendranagar, in Surkhet district. It is located in a small valley in the Terai region, surrounded by hills. I was to stay there for three weeks to interview people affected by leprosy. Whenever I told anyone in Kathmandu that I was going there, they were aghast. It was March/April and pre-monsoon and so hot, especially in the Terai region– too hot for even many Nepalese at that time of the year. I must admit that their comments put the wind up me. I do not cope well in hot climates. Even in Kathmandu I sweat profusely. I constantly have a flannel in my hand, wiping the sweat off my face. My hair at the front is always wet from sweat and my face is like a red balloon. Not a pretty picture! Whenever I go into a shop, the shopkeepers rush to put the fan on and get me a stool. I would like to think that it is out of politeness, but I think that it is because I look as if I will pass out at any second. Anyway, I must keep to the point. I decided that I would fly to Birendranagar. It was 233 miles to fly and 362 miles by road. This told me that there was not a straight route by road between the two and judging by other road journeys I had already done, that spelt a long and uncomfortable trip. I went to the internal flight booking office. It was total Bedlam. People, men mainly, were pushing and shuffling to get to the metal grill to buy tickets to one of the remote domestic airports. There seemed to be no system at all. The Germanic side of me took over. I decided not to get in the non-existent queue and battled my way through the throng. I think people were so surprised that I was doing this and so let me through. The ticket seller was not as accommodating. I asked for a one-way ticket to Birendranagar. All the planes are full, he claimed. Someone whispered in my ear, "offer to pay in dollars". I did. I took dollars out of my purse and waved them at him. Lo and behold there was a seat available the very next day. Success!

The next day I flew to Birendranagar. It took about an hour by a 20-seater small plane. As I got off the plane, I was hit by the intense pre-monsoon heat and humidity. I felt wet, my clothes were sticking to me and yet my mouth was parched. I was not sure if I would survive the next three weeks, but I obviously did. It never ceases to amaze me how much a body can tolerate.

I was shown to the guest house that was owned by the organisation I was to be based at. This was to be my home during my stay. There was no-one in the guest house when I arrived, but a note had been left for me to help myself to food. I looked in the kitchen cupboards and one was full of Tupperware containers. I could not believe it. I later met the woman who looked after the house. She was from New Zealand, hence the Tupperware.

I have decided not to share my experiences of being in the town because it was mostly talking to people affected by leprosy which was, at times, intrusive and always confidential. Suffice to say the whole experience was extremely interesting, humbling and soul-searching. I met people who shared their intimate stories of courage and survival beyond belief.

My three weeks passed quite quickly although I was constantly drained by the heat. I had not made any plans for my return journey, except that I wanted to go to Pokhara to visit my Nepali friend and to visit the leprosy hospital there. I assumed that I could get a flight to Pokhara, or at least a bus. On the map it looked to be about 110 miles due east. Well, no planes flew to Pokhara from Birendranagar, just to Kathmandu and to some very remote villages in the mountains. Road it was then! Oh, dear me, when I looked at the map, I had failed to see that between us and Pokhara were hills, high hills, and no road.

It turned out that there was only one road out of Birendranagar, and that went south to Nepalgunj on the Indian border. Luckily, a couple of men from the organisation I was involved with were going to Nepalgunj the next day and I accepted their kind offer of a lift. There was a bus from Nepalgunj that evening which would then take me directly to Pokhara. Perfect! We left Birendranagar early the next morning by land-rover. The road was bumpy, but I had been on worse. The journey was four hours, which wasn't too bad for a 61-mile trip, and the route was remarkably interesting. We drove through Bardia National Park where I saw my first jackals, lots of monkeys and scores of vultures. Indeed, the expedition was quite pleasurable.

When we arrived in Nepalgunj one of men helped me to book my bus to Pokhara and left. I had six hours to kill. What should I do? I did as most people in that position would do, I went to visit the local hospital where I was told leprosy patients were treated. It was a small hospital, mainly a general hospital but also treated people in the area with leprosy. I was shown around by a Swiss physiotherapist who had been put in charge of the hospital despite not even being a doctor. A nice man.

As he took me from each department to another, we met a local man in the corridor. He was clutching his stomach and looked extremely uncomfortable. In his hand he was holding what looked like a piece of cling film. The man was pleading with the 'doctor' to look at what he had brought. I asked what he wanted. The physiotherapist said that he had brought in his worm to show him that he had passed that morning: "People are always doing that". With that the man opened his package and looked horrified. It had gone. He had lost the worm on the way. We spent the next ten minutes walking up and down the corridors looking for his lost worm. Alas, it had slithered off.

I arrived at the bus park to catch the 7 pm coach to Pokhara. It was the luxury tourist overnight coach, so I was full of high expectations. I am an optimist if nothing else. My rucksack was heaved onto the roof of the coach with dozens of sacks of rice, colourful blankets in Perspex bags and even a TV. All seats were allocated, and I was given one near to the front and in the aisle. A local woman was sitting next to me. She went to sleep as soon as her head touched the window. The seats were reasonably comfortable, and I was so looking forward to winding back my backrest to have a sleep. All the seats seemed to be taken and I noticed that I was the only non-Nepali on the coach. I was used to being the odd one out and being stared at all the time. Two women got on the coach, just across from me. They were carrying two small crates of chickens. The chickens were not happy about their imprisonment and were flapping around and squealing. I couldn't fathom out where the women were going to put them. All seats were taken. Silly me. They were put in the overhead luggage rack, of course.

Off we set, remarkably almost keeping to time. Very soon I began to get the sense that life on the coach may not be as luxurious as promised. The man sitting in front of me wound down his backrest until it was literally on my lap. He lay back with his hands over his head and went to sleep. It was an overnight coach, so I suppose that it was the sensible thing to do. However, my backrest did not move, it was solid and was going nowhere. I had to sit bolt upright for the whole journey. I must admit as time went on, I childishly deliberately knocked his hands on more than one occasion in the hope of him waking and sitting up. But, no, he was dead to the world.

We had only been on the road for about 30 minutes when we stopped. Standing by the side of the road were about three men and a flock of goats, about six. Naively I thought they were waiting to cross the road. Suddenly the luggage compartment under the coach was opened and two goats were lifted in, and the door shut. To say I was astounded was an understatement. Next the other goats were lifted somehow onto the top of the coach and tethered to the roof. The men joined them. I was lost for words. Selfishly, my first thought was "I hope the goats don't pee on my rucksack". We set off again.

We had several short stops on the way, mainly for toilet needs and to trim off the frayed rubber from the tyres. The roads were very poorly constructed and even crumbly which shredded the tyres. The driver looked no older than 12 years with an even younger looking assistant. The assistant's job was to hang out of the coach door and whistle when directing the coach along hillside roads. Along most of the route, there was a drop down the side of the road of many feet. There was much evidence of the demise of wrecked and burnt-out coaches and lorries at the bottom of the ravines. So, our lives were in the hands of a young lad who whistled when the wheels got too near the edge of the road. Comforting? No.

Added to this it was getting increasingly dark. There were no markings or lights on the road. Some people were looking genuinely concerned and there was often an intake of breath when we went round a hairpin bend. Not sure how the goats were getting on. Unbelievably, I was not afraid. I tried to blinker myself from dodgy situations. So, I never looked out of the window on the side of dangerous drops. Ignorance, in situations where you have no control, is always bliss!

The journey was extremely long. It took more than seventeen hours. Long parts of it were boring, especially in the dark but were punctuated by little incidents. One such ray of light was when the coach made a sharp swerve which caused the chickens in the overhead rack to break free from their captivity and flap around the coach. They were screeching and the feathers and greenish chicken poo were flying everywhere. There were a lot of arms flaying, shouting and screaming coming from the other passengers as the owners tried to catch them. I was in hysterics with laughter. You couldn't make it up. It was one of the funniest incidents I had seen for a long time. But I did wonder how the goat passengers were getting along and whether they had peed or, even worse, pooped on my rucksack.

As we approached the outskirts of Pokhara our 'luxury' came to a total end. It was time for the driver to supplement his income by extending the coach service to others. The goats were taken off the roof. Their transportation had given the driver additional cash. They were replaced with people clambering on the roof – lots of people. Inside the coach became a heaving sea of, men, women, and children. They were sitting or standing on every imaginable space, the gangway, the steps of the coach, hanging out of the door, everywhere. When those spaces were filled, they sat where no spaces were, such as on the original passengers. I had at least three children thrust onto my lap – the man had woken up by then and put his seat in the upright position. It was total chaos and not very pleasant. These extra passengers jumped off the coach just before the bus park so the boss wouldn't know. I suspect that the driver could only get away with that for a short while before he was rumbled. At least he made a few extra rupees which was the nature of the game. We arrived at Pokhara 17 hours after we set off from Nepalgunj. My rucksack had survived the journey and had stayed dry. It was an interesting experience but one I do not want to repeat.

My trips to Ghandruk, in the early days, were only possible by foot. My body is not designed for such exertion and each time I arrived in Ghandruk I was utterly amazed that I had survived. I also know that anyone who had accompanied me was amazed that I had survived. It did nothing for my self-esteem. I used to watch other people trekking along the route with ease, which made me extremely envious. Ok, many were much younger than me or built like goats. The local people were obviously used to the terrain, yet it was not much comfort to me to watch very elderly women striding along at great speed, often carrying heavy loads of firewood or animal fodder in a doko – a straw basket that was carried by a strap on the forehead. Likewise, it did not bolster my confidence when a man, about 4'10", with broken flip-flops ascended the trail with 100 coke bottles on his back. Indeed, my confidence plummeted to new levels when a blind elderly woman once took my hand to guide me down the trail because she was worried that I would slip.

However, on my first visit to Ghandruk I met someone who shared my dislike of walking and seemed to have the same fitness level. I was just getting over dysentery. This was something I caught several times over my many visits to Nepal. It was quiet in the village as it was out of season, so whenever a trekker walked past the lodge where I was staying, I would greet them and invite them for tea. I wanted familiar conversation as I was still feeling sorry for myself. Sometimes my invitations were accepted, and we had a nice time, other times I was looked at as if I was a mad woman. One day a Japanese couple arrived at the lodge to stay. They were about my age and as soon as the woman saw me, she said "I thought that I was going to die. That walk up to here was impossible. I am not going any higher". At last, a kindred spirit! We spent many cups of coffee over the next couple of days, decrying the challenges of trekking. I felt much better, especially when she shared some processed cheese she had brought from Japan.

No one had warned me about walking downhill. I should have realised that downhill trekking was equally challenging as walking uphill, if not worse. The problem with the trail is that it is not regular like stairs. One step could be six inches high and the next two-feet, and the next one-foot. Some of the trail is a bit wobbly or slippery. So, there was no chance of getting a regular rhythm whilst going up or down. As usual, I learnt the hard way just how exhausting going downhill actually is.

It was time for me to leave Ghandruk after a couple of incredible weeks working in a children's nursery and becoming immersed in the Gurung culture. The Gurungs were the ethnic group that are predominant in the village and surrounding areas. The night before my departure I met a couple of men who were working for the environmental organisation based in the village. They were leaving the village themselves the next day and would have transport waiting for them in Naya Pul to take them to Pokhara. I accepted their offer of a lift. They suggested that I set off downhill an hour before they did because I would be slower than them. My new-found empowerment turned into stroppiness. Huh, just because I am a woman. I will show them. Gravity will take me down quicker. Huh.

The next morning, however, I did set off early, on my own. Many of the villagers had come out to say good-bye and layered me with lots of flower mallas, scarves and tikka to wish me luck. I was overcome with their generosity. Such wonderful people. I kept the adornments around my neck to show how grateful I was. The first half of the journey was ok. My fitness levels had grown with many jaunts around the village. I was feeling particularly good about myself. I was bathing in wonderful memories of my time in Ghandruk. What a joy! Then my legs started to wobble, and I started to stumble, as I did when walking up. I began to have bad feelings about the rest of the journey. I heard running behind me and saw the men from the night before running down the hillside at a fast pace and past me. They laughed at my distress. Off they ran into the distance, calling that they would see me in Naya Pul.

I struggled, really struggled on, my legs getting more and more shaky and my pride diminishing by the step. Every ounce of energy had dissolved. I had nothing left. I was so hot. I lay on the path with my flannel over my face. I could hear my Japanese friend's words, "I thought that I was going to die". I knew exactly how she felt. I lay there, thinking about how my family would react to my demise. Suddenly the flannel was taken off my face. A local woman had arrived, I thought she was an angel. I think she thought I was a corpse. On either side of the path were rice fields. My angel dipped the flannel in the water where the rice was growing, and carefully lay it on my face. It felt so good, it was cool. She sat with me on the path and replenished my flannel until I felt that I should move, even if it was to prove to my angel that I was not dead. She helped me up onto my feet and kept hold of my arm as we walked together along the remains of the trail. A couple of local men came towards us and offered to carry me. I had just enough pride left to decline the offer.

Amazingly, the men and transport were still waiting for me. I was several hours late. They were obviously extremely amused by the state I was in. My angel held my hand and helped me into the land rover. I thanked her profusely, sank back in my seat and cried. Never again!

I was driven to a hotel in Pokhara that had been recommended to me. One of the men went into the hotel to check there was a room. He came out with two beautiful hotel maids who helped me out of the car. Each one took an arm and guided me up the steps of the hotel and into my bedroom. I was like a zombie. I could hardly move. One of the maids filled my bath with water and they left me to it.

Every bone and muscle in my body hurt especially my legs and back. Somehow, I managed to get undressed and slither into the bath. I soaked my body for a long time, my mind going over the events of the day. I must be mad. Why am I doing these things? I must have dozed off because the water was cold, and it was going dark. With every ounce of my strength, I clambered out of the bath. I was still hurting but at least I was beginning to feel I was actually alive.

The following year, and being a glutton for punishment, I went back to the village. I had a visit that can only be described as what dreams are made of. I worked in the nursery and did research into women's development issues for my independent study for my degree. I really got into the swing of cultural life and was honoured at one of the women's meetings I attended by having my name changed to a Gurung name. The women could not pronounce my name 'Janet' so they decided I was to be given a name they could say. I became an honorary Gurung because I tried to dress like a Gurung, in traditional clothes, I tried to talk like a Gurung, albeit very poorly and I laughed like a Gurung. They had the most incredible, if not twisted, sense of humour. I discovered early on that I needed a sense of humour to get along in Nepal. I was given the name Sita. I said I was pleased as it was the name of a god, so very appropriate for me and it was short enough for me to pronounce. We had a ceremony with lots of flower mallas, tikka, flower posies and laughter. As I have said, my time there was magical.

My journey, as I left the village, was as torturous as the previous year, but I was helped by my porter. I was terribly slow and my transport at the other end did not wait for me this time. Naya Pul, in those days, was a small village that was the main kerosene depot for the surrounding area, with a few rickety tea shops, and small general shops. The sun was going down, and my porter had to leave me to go back up to Ghandruk. I was on my own. There were occasional buses that went to Pokhara and sometimes taxis, but this time no taxis, and the last bus had gone. Oh, dear me, what to do? I was still basking in my magical experiences of this visit and had adopted too much of the Nepali culture of fatalism. It will all be OK. With that I sat on a step and just sat. I was not worried. I was not afraid to be stuck there. Perhaps I had gone mad.

Suddenly, a young lad of about 14 years old ran up to me and said that he had got me transport back to Pokhara. I had not seen him before, but he had run onto the main road to look for someone to take me back. So incredibly kind. He had stopped a lorry with four men inside the cab. The Nepali lorries, like Indian ones, are very ornate with brightly coloured pictures of gods or animals painted on them. Often, they were adorned with tinsel or bunting. Unfortunately, many are also very poorly maintained, with frayed or bald tyres and doors held on with string or Sellotape. The young lad asked if I minded going in a lorry and I jumped at the chance. I had not been in a lorry since I used to hitch in the 60s to dances in the Derbyshire Dales.

Getting into a cab with four unknown men did not faze me as I had a rape alarm on me. I had bought one with me because I had to go through a jungle area on my way to Ghandruk, so I thought a rape alarm would keep me safe. See how naïve I was? As I climbed in the cab, the pin of the alarm came out and it started to screech – ear piercingly loud. The men laughed and I put the pin back in to stop it. I put it in my bag and sat back in my seat. I did not speak Nepali and they did not speak English, but we had some interesting conversations on the way. The men dropped me off in Pokhara. Such a remarkable experience, although stupidly risky!

On one of my later visits to Ghandruk I had a change of mode of transport. I nearly did not venture up as I had been advised by a doctor not to walk up there as I had high blood pressure. However, I was keen to get into the hills, even if was only part way. There is something replenishing about being deep in the countryside, especially after a few days of noisy and polluted Kathmandu. I decided to walk part way and assess the situation. I would walk as far as Sauli Bazaar which was about a third of the way and relatively flat compared to the rest of journey.

Initially I had to get to Naya Pul from Pokhara, which is about 30 miles away. I got a taxi from the town to the bus park just outside Pokhara. It was early in the morning, but it was busy with lots of buses and taxis. Nepal was very much a 'morning' place. My next job was to find a taxi that was going to Naya Pul. I wandered from one taxi to another asking the drivers where they were going. No joy. Eventually I heard someone call out "Naya Pul, Naya Pul". I followed the sound to a taxi right in the middle of the mayhem of transport. It had someone in the back, in fact two people. The driver said he would take me to Naya Pul in his 'share taxi'. The idea is that as many people as possible climb into the taxi and share the fare. I can do that.

I was invited to jump into the front seat. The joy of being much bigger than the average Nepali! That left space in the back for at least two more passengers. In climbed a man and a woman who was heavily pregnant. She had to sit on someone's knee. I must admit that I felt guilty for having so much room to myself at the front, but I soon got over it. The drive to Naya Pul was beautiful. The joy of the monsoon period is that everywhere is lush and green, and the waterfalls are in full flow. We travelled into the foothills, with stunning views of the Fishtail Mountain and the Annapurnas. Up, up, up, we went then down, down, down to the river side. The journey took about an hour.

My porter was waiting for me at Naya Pul. He was holding up a piece of paper with 'Sita Gurung' written on it. I was thrilled that I was known by my Gurung name. After strapping my rucksack and other bags on his back we set off. As soon as we started to walk, I knew that Sauli Bazaar would be the end of my journey. There was no way I could walk up to the village. However, I had many goods to get to Ghandruk. Ladies at my local church had knit many blankets and clothes for the children at the nursery after I had given a talk to them about Nepal. I knew that the children would benefit greatly from them.

When we reached Sauli Bazaar, I checked into a room in a small guest house. I sorted out what needed to go to Ghandruk, especially the knitwear, and what was to stay with me. I wrote a note to my Nepali friend, Jagan, in Ghandruk explaining my health situation and telling her that I would stay in Sauli Bazaar for two days if she wanted to come down to see me. I had a large amount of money to give her from fundraising by my daughter and myself for the nursery. I would hang onto it and give it to her if she could come down. I sent the porter off with the goods and note and went to have a siesta in my room. I was so relieved that I didn't have to do that walk.

The rest of the day was very pleasant. I relaxed, read, and became at one with nature, just enjoying listening to the birds and insects and the lack of anything mechanical. Everywhere smelt fresh. The guest house was really comfortable, exceptionally clean. There was no electricity but that was not a problem, there was a feeling of safety and peace.

Three Russian men arrived in the late afternoon and invited me to join them for a cup of tea that they made on a portable paraffin stove. That is one of the many joys of travelling, especially in Nepal, that you meet such an array of people from all over the world. Indeed, later we were joined by two Israeli girls. Nationality, gender and age do not seem to be a barrier during these sorts of trips. Most people get along with each other. Perhaps it is because they know that they will not see each other again.

I went to bed and fell asleep knowing that I would not have to walk up to Ghandruk. At six o'clock there was a commotion outside my room, laughter, shouting. The Nepalese do sometimes shout when they talk. I thought that the trekkers were setting off. Suddenly there was a bang on my door. Obviously got the wrong door. Bang, bang again. I opened the door to see a small one-eyed man standing there. "Ghandruk, you go to Ghandruk" he said. "No, you've got it wrong. I am not going to Ghandruk. I am sick. I cannot walk up there". "You go by horse". "No, I didn't order a horse." With that he fetched a mule. The mule was standing on three legs, obviously lame and was dripping wet with sweat. "Jagan said that you go by horse". What the....!!!! Jagan had hired the mule to take me up to Ghandruk. "Jagan said you must go". Crumbs. No one argued with Jagan. I gave in. Now my experiences with horses/donkeys/mules were limited. I used to enjoy riding on the donkeys at Blackpool when I was a child. Who didn't? But I was put on a real horse when I was in my early teens, and it bolted. I have been extremely wary of them since. Jagan must have really wanted me to go. It would be rude for me to refuse her offer.

The Russian men helped me to get on the mule. Everyone seemed to find my trepidation amusing. I was absolutely petrified. We set off, the mule man (I will call him Ram) guiding his charge and me clinging onto the reins for dear life. Within a few hundred yards we started to climb the steep steps. I was leaning back, which was strangling the mule. "Forward, forward" screamed Ram. He wanted me to lean on the neck of the mule (let's call him Neddy) while going up. I did as I was told. Sometimes we would go down to cross the streams. This was really frightening because I then had to lean back but felt that I was going to slide down Neddy's neck and head. Sometimes I would just get off Neddy and walk down and join him on the other side of the stream.

There were many tea shops along the trail. Our 'routine' was that when we reached a tea shop, I would get off Neddy. This would give him a rest which he needed. He held his leg up and sweated so much that there was pool of water around him. I felt so sorry for him. I was no lightweight and because I had to snuggle up to his neck for so long, I was getting quite attached. Ram and I would have a cold drink and then we would set off again.

We had trodden quite a way when we came to another tea shop. Both Neddy and I were relieved. Neddy started to turn towards the tea shop. I sat upright. Ram had other ideas. He pulled the reins to carry on up the steps. Neddy jolted onto the next step, I lost concentration, and as he set off up another step I fell back – right off the back of Neddy. I landed flat on my back on the steps. The steps had sharp edges and we were on the part of the trail where there was a drop of many feet. I lay there in shock. I felt some pain in my back but also my hip and legs. I taught about health and development in developing countries at the university so was aware of the difficulties of getting help here. There was no way of getting a helicopter to me. My mind was working overtime. I will be in a wheelchair. My house will have to be adapted. Who will do the cooking? Would I be able to drive? Could I carry on teaching? How would I get to the toilet? Strange how the brain works. People say that your past life flashes in front of your eyes if you think you are going to die. In my case, the thought of permanent injury made me think of my potential future. I am not sure who was more worried, me or Ram.

Yet, I had to move. I could not stay on that path for ever. It was a busy route for not only locals and trekkers, but buffalo and trains of mules carrying supplies. I did not want to be trampled to death. I started to get up, very gingerly. Ram and a village girl helped me to my feet and lay me on a bed that was in the tea shop. My back did not seem too bad, considering the whack it had had. I was carrying a small rucksack on my back, and I believe that it broke my fall. Ram started to rub my leg while the village girl took the other. I then rested flat on the bed for a while.

Remarkably when I got up, I just had pains in my left hip and leg. I was so lucky. There was also nothing else to do but to get back on Neddy. I certainly couldn't possibly walk up to Ghandruk now. Ram held onto me as he walked by the side of Neddy and me. We went at a slower pace. By then I was petrified of riding Neddy, especially when his back hoof often stumbled off the edge of the drop. My inner child took over and I whimpered and screamed whenever I felt the slightest threat to my safety which was most of the time. We eventually arrived in Ghandruk and was met by my worried friend. News carries fast in the hills. I played down my experience as I didn't want Jagan to feel guilty.

47

After all it was my incompetence on horseback that caused my fall not because she had sent a mule out of kindness for me. The next day was extremely painful. The bruises came out and my muscles ached on every part of my body. One of the village men arrived with a walking stick which he made especially for me. Everyone is so kind. I spent the rest of my time in Ghandruk limping around. Needless to say, when it was time to depart, I definitely did not want to go by mule and chose to walk down, very slowly with my walking stick. Each step was tortuous, and I had to lean heavily on my porter. He was sweet but wanted me to teach him English along the way. It was the last thing I wanted but the least I could do.

The rest of my visit to Nepal was spent with me using my walking stick. I was still in pain, mainly my hip and leg but at least I was alive and not confined to a wheelchair. This all happened when I was researching for my PhD. On my return to Kathmandu, I went to the leprosy shelter where most of my research was conducted. It was located next to the local cremation temple. I had built up a friendship with the staff and some of the patients, so I enjoyed hanging around there in my spare time.

I was still using my walking stick and walking with a limp. I took up my favourite spot on a low wall at the front of the shelter. People who were attending cremations or tourists visiting the cremation temple had to walk past, so for me being a voyeur or people watcher it was perfect. Sometimes I would try and converse with the people affected by leprosy or just sit and have a coffee with them. Many had gross deformities of their feet or hands. Some had no fingers or had disfigurement of their face. Yet they were coming to me with drinks and to rub my back or leg. I felt so humbled. Unfortunately, I had to move from my prime position. Marianne, the German owner of the shelter, came up to me and said, "Janet, I know you like sitting there but with your injuries and limping, you are giving leprosy a bad name. Please move so no one can see you!". Direct or what!!!!!

Several years later a road was built along the trail, not quite reaching Ghandruk but a place called Kimche. This was two-thirds of the way to Ghandruk. The final stage of about one and a half hours was by foot only. Most times when I visited Nepal the road was impassable or at least too dangerous because of the monsoon rains, and so I didn't venture up. However, a few years ago Jagan said that the road was clear, and we should go and see the village again. It had been such a long time since the last visit. Claire had died since then and, whilst Jagan kept me up to date with the news of the projects supported by Claire's Memorial fund, it would be nice to see them in action. So, we set off on our journey.

Initially we needed to get a four-wheel-drive vehicle to tackle the road. Even buses went up, but there was no way I would risk that. Unfortunately, there were no 4x4s available. Jagan decided to take an ordinary taxi. I always put my trust in Jagan. We found one, but it looked a bit battered. I put my bags in the boot and we got in it. An elderly man who had been a Gurkha soldier and lived in Ghandruk also joined us. The taxi did not start. This did not bode well. I had a lot of experience of cars not starting and having to be push-started. My dad's cars were often like that. The driver tried to turn the engine several times but no go, so it was pushed to start. At last, we were off. We drove to Naya Pul, stopped off at the local school to see two young girls who Claire's fund was supporting for their education, and carried on again. When I had previously been to Naya Pul it was like a scene from a western film, very sparsely populated and built. Now it was like a small town with brightly coloured shops, guest houses, lorries, buses, and pollution. I suppose that is 'development'.

We had only been travelling for fifteen minutes when we reached our first obstacle. Well, I thought it was, but the driver didn't. You judge. It was a river and about three feet deep. This will be interesting, I thought. I couldn't believe it; we drove right into the river. We got about half-way and stopped. No surprise there. The water was coming through the floor. I lifted my feet. Then it was coming in through the badly sealed doors. The water eventually reached my waist. My knickers were wet through, indeed everything.

The driver, Jagan and the ex-Gurkha got out of the taxi. I was told to stay put. I was going nowhere. I couldn't swim anyway. The ex-Gurkha took control. He must have been used to rescuing people out of rivers. By now we had been joined by some children and men who were swimming in the river. Everyone tried to push the taxi. It too was going nowhere. I did as anyone would have done; I took out my camera which was in my small bag that I was holding above my head so as not to get wet. I knew that no one would believe me back home that I was sitting in a taxi in a river, in the Himalayas with water past my waist, so I had to show them some evidence. Click, click, I took some images of our ordeal. At one point the children who were pushing the car, stopped to pose for a photo. That was not what I intended. I didn't want it to look like a jolly. Eventually a 4x4 appeared on the other side of the river and after a lot of toing and froing it pulled the taxi – and me- out of the water. And miracles of all miracles the car engine started first time. There was a lot of cheering by everyone, and we set off again.

Whilst the road was clear by Nepali standards, it would not win any awards anywhere else. It was wide enough for only about one and a half vehicles to pass each other The surface was very rutted, potholed and, at times, resembled a lunar landscape, made worse by the heavy traffic and the monsoon rains.

In order to add to the 'interest' of the journey, the road was semi-blocked by a number of landslides. However, a minor detail like a landslide did not stop this intrepid driver as he would just take a run, in the taxi of course, and we would get over the rubble. One such time, he took at least eight runs to get over a particularly large and tricky one. That would have been bad enough but there was a very deep sheer drop at the side of the road, so his positioning when hitting the landslide was crucial to our survival. But we made it! At last, we arrived in Kimche, wet but alive. I had walked through Kimche several times, it had been a couple of guest houses and tea shops. Now there was a car/bus park and several brick-built restaurants/guest houses. I couldn't make my mind up as to whether all this development was a good or bad change for the area. But who was I to judge?

After a meal of dal bhat (lentils and rice) it was time for us to finish the rest of the journey to Ghandruk. By now I had had sciatica for a few years, so walking was out of the question -again. The only way was by a dreaded mule. Marley was brought to me, and we were introduced. He looked as pleased to see me as I was to see him. It was time to go. I couldn't put off the moment any longer. As I stood next to Marley, a very old lady was carried past me. Her ambulance was a large doko basket carried by a young slightly built man. She was going to Ghandruk after being in hospital. She looked so happy. I felt so pathetic and ungrateful of being frightened of riding a mule.

"OK, how do I get on this", I asked the mule man. "You swing your leg over its back", he said. I tried. No joy. "Jump and throw your body and then your leg over". Still no joy. "I can't lift my leg over, can't you see?" By then I had created a live performance of how not to get on a mule. My audience of several dozen local people were laughing at my poor drama skills. Then everyone joined in, offering their own tips on how to do it. I had picked up a few Nepali words over the years, one such word was 'moto' which means fat. I heard that a few times during their 'encouragement'. It's a good job that I am used to being humiliated in public in Nepal or I could have been scarred for life. We moved to a shop veranda that was nearly level with Marley's back. Yes, I managed it. I got my leg over Marley, put my feet in the stirrups and settled onto the 'saddle' which was a wooden frame covered by a mat. I also put my rain poncho on as the heavens had opened and off we set. I hope my spectators felt that they had had value for money.

Jagan walked on one side of me and the mule man, Bob, I have named him, walked on the other side holding me on with one hand. I felt extremely uncomfortable as I seemed to be leaning over to one side. Bob kept pushing me back. After only a few minutes he instructed me to take off my poncho as he could not see how far my body was tilting. I think that by now he could see that my riding skills were downright dangerous. I was still drenched through from the taxi episode so removing my poncho in the rain would not make much difference to my overall wetness.

The journey to Ghandruk seemed to be endless but was only about one to two hours. I can honestly say I was petrified all the way. What was I doing? I was in my sixties, a grandmother and playing at Indiana Jones. I must be mad. I'm too old for all this. My inner child came out again as I whimpered every time Marley's hoof lost his footing. I hung onto Marley's mane for dear life, my hands really hurting from the desperate grip I was using. I clenched my hips and knees so tightly so as not to fall off Marley. And I prayed. I prayed to every god in the world. I became a Buddhist, Hindu, Sheikh, Jain and Muslim as well as staying a Christian for good luck. I begged Claire to look after me and keep me safe. (I actually think that she would be laughing her head off really). Whenever we went up or down the steps, I closed my eyes tightly. Yes, ignorance is bliss. At last, I could see the familiar buildings of Ghandruk. We are alive. The relief was indescribable. I nearly cried with happiness. Bob and Marley took me to Jagan's lodge. Home at last! I felt Bob and Jagan's relief that I had survived.

Marley was steered to the courtyard of the lodge. He was positioned against a bench so I could climb off him. Oh, dear me. I was as stiff as a board. My fingers had to be prised open to let go of Marley's mane. My back, legs and feet were so stiff and painful I couldn't move them. I managed to mumble, "How do I get off?". "Swing your leg over," said Bob. I tried but was unable to move. "Swing your leg over, didi". Bob said again. "But I have told you before I can't swing my leg over, it won't move", snapped my 9-year-old inner child. I am stuck on here for ever, I thought. Suddenly four men grabbed hold of me and just pulled me off Marley. I was dismounted unceremoniously. It was the only way with me.

Jagan's sister-in-law, who managed the lodge for her, took my arm and led me to my usual room. Since my last visit, Jagan had expanded the lodge and some rooms, including mine, had *en*-suite bathrooms. Luxury. I had a lovely hot shower and opened my holdall to get out some nice clean dry clothes. Oh no. Every item of clothing was wet through. They had been in the boot of the taxi and the river had risen above the boot, hence everything in it got sodden. I had literally nothing dry to wear. What to do? I couldn't spend my time in Ghandruk wearing only a towel. Even I have standards. I put on wet, but at least clean underwear – sorry if that is too much information – a t-shirt that seemed slightly drier than my others and a village girl loaned me a lungi. A lungi is a traditional wrap over skirt that will fit most sizes of individual. I hung the rest of my clothes on a line outside my room to dry. I was there for five days but nothing dried because of the monsoon clouds and dampness. But I managed. I did dry some pants on the rice cooker in the kitchen, overnight. Where there is a will there is a way.

Suffice to say when it was time to leave the village, I walked down to Kimche and travelled by taxi back to

Pokhara. The river that we got stuck in was slightly lower and the taxi managed to doggy-paddle through, although we did need a push for the last bit. As we hit the water, I stood up and hitched up my skirt. The water only came to my knees this time, so I was able to prevent a soaking and my holdall, containing half dry clothes, was strapped to the roof. These experiences are given to us to learn from. This lesson was 'how to drive through a river and not get your clothes wet'.

One of the most 'exciting' journeys I have taken in Nepal was the one I experienced when I was going to the airport to make my return flight back the UK after my first visit to Nepal. I was told that there was going to be a national strike or Banda the next day. These Bandas were called often and at short notice. I cannot remember the reason for this one, but they are usually political, or student led. During the Banda, which can last hours or days or even weeks, everything comes to a halt or is closed. Therefore, all shops are closed, and all transport, including private transport, is forbidden on the road. If caught the perpetrator can be beaten or have their vehicle taken off them or burnt. I was flying home at about mid-day on the next day so how was I going to get to the airport? I, obviously, was not the only person in this predicament. Huddles of people were found on the streets of Thamel plotting their 'escape'. I don't know who organised the plan but by that evening we were given the final details.

I left my hotel at about 4am. It was pitch dark and I had to wake up the staff at the hotel who were sleeping on the floor in the lobby to move them from the door that they were blocking. I had arranged for a cycle rickshaw to pick me up from the hotel. We had to leave at that time as it was a little safer than leaving after 7am when the protesters usually are in full force. I had to pay the rickshaw driver danger money, way above the odds. But needs must. I loaded my big rucksack and hand luggage onto the seat and somehow managed to find a space for me to sit. We set off for Hotel Annapurna. This rendezvous was only about 20 minutes cycle away but the driver and me were constantly looking around for any sign of protesters. It was really eerie, yet exciting, going through empty streets in the dark on a silent rickshaw, knowing we could be in potential danger. I climbed off the rickshaw when we arrived at the hotel. There were several people waiting outside with all their baggage. Some looked really nervous. More and more people arrived by rickshaw. The tension mounted.

Suddenly our transport arrived for the next part of the journey, to take us to the airport. It was a large army security van. The windows were meshed and there were bullet-proof shields attached to the bodywork. There were soldiers on the roof with guns. We were loaded inside the van. There were no seats, so we had to stand up, with our bags. We were crammed in, shoulder to shoulder. At one point I was worried that I was going to fall over but that physically could not happen as I couldn't move. By that time, the protesters had realised we were fleeing. As we reached the end of the road there was a large group of them, waiting for us. They were shouting and banging on the sides of the van. Then stones were hurled. Some of the passengers started to cry. I am not sure why I wasn't frightened. Perhaps I was naïve or just mad, but I had confidence in the protection of the van, and I had never heard of any tourists being hurt in these Bandas. At each road junction we were greeted with a few protesters, throwing stones and jeering.

The journey to the airport was remarkably quick, no other vehicles on the road and the speed of the van helped. I must admit I was glad to get off as it was getting extremely hot and uncomfortable in there. At last, we were outside the airport, dozens of people who were all for my flight. Now you would have expected that we could all go inside the building, for safety and comfort, but no. The airport does not open until three hours before the flight out and a little matter of worried tourists who have had to escape from violent protesters would not prompt the authorities to have pity on us. Consequently, we all had to stand outside for several hours until the doors opened. What an end to an incredible initial visit to Nepal!

Where is the rhino?

Ever since I was a child I had always wanted to go on safari. I loved animals and the thought of seeing 'exotic' ones in the wild was so exciting. So, when I saw the posters in Pokhara advertising safaris in Nepal I decided that I should go on one. The time of year was not the best, as I have said before, I tend to go to Nepal during the monsoon period, but the two nights, three days all-in trip to an island jungle in Chitwan National Park was a ridiculous price, something like £100 or even less. That included transport to the park, all meals, accommodation, and activities. I always liked a bargain. Chitwan was an area in southern Nepal, close to the Indian border. It was in the Inner Terai, one of the valleys in the flat part of Nepal. Hence, it was guaranteed to be hot. I had been to Nepal several times by now and concluded that if my body temperature gauge was to rule my life then I may as well not bother doing anything. So, if I was physically fit to do something that other people were doing I would do it. After all, other people coped so why should I be different? I booked the trip for the next day before I could change my mind.

A coach collected me from my hotel in Pokhara early in the next morning. There were lots of other non-Nepalis on the coach so I thought that I would have a lot of company on the safari. Off we set. We travelled for several hours. The environment started to become even more rural, if that was possible in rural Nepal, with small hamlets and compounds. The petite thatched houses were home to families getting along with their daily business. Children were playing and women were washing the clothes in a steel bowl filled by water from a hosepipe or a stream of water running down the road. The clothes were hung to dry on any convenient bush or low tree. Often women and children could be seen having a full-body wash down at the stream. Whilst this could be viewed by all, the people are very modest and were careful not to expose themselves, by wearing a lungi or towel.

Most houses had animals of some sort. Many had at least one buffalo, tethered to a pole or allowed to roam freely onto the road. Buffalo are especially important to Nepali families as they provided milk, dung and pulled simple ploughs to till the fields. Eventually they become a source of meat and hide. The coach had to swerve many times around a delinquent buffalo and wandering ducks or hens. Many people also had a goat or two. I hated to see them outside shops as I knew that they were there to be slaughtered. They would stand in a line and could not avoid watching the front one from being decapitated. The other ones must have been so frightened.

What I did find interesting was the drying of the chillies or grains. They were spread out on a nanglo (bamboo round tray) or sheet and placed in the middle of the road as that was where the sun is at its warmest, of course. I kept my window open to let out the stifling heat of the coach, only to be replaced by exhaust fumes, smells of cooking and manure, and occasionally the sweet fragrance of the tropical vegetation. I preferred the onslaught on my nostrils to the debilitating heat on my body.

We eventually stopped in the town of Narayanghat where I alighted; just me. The rest of the passengers stayed put, they must have been going to India or another safari resort. Oh well, I went most places on my own so that was OK. I was directed to a hotel along the main road of the town. It was very pretty with neatly cultivated gardens. I accepted a meal of rice and some sort of vegetable curry that was served in an elegant dining room. The meal was nice, the surroundings were nice, but I was a little deflated that this was to be my safari location. It was supposed to be on an island. I was in the middle of a town, what animals could I see from here? I had been promised elephant rides and crocodile walks. I had been conned. I wanted excitement not 'nice'. Suddenly, a man arrived and told me that we would be going in a few minutes. "Where?" I asked. "To the safari resort, of course". Oh dear, I really had got it all wrong.

There was a jeep waiting outside. Now the action starts, I thought. I always fancied travelling in a real jeep. Another man joined us with, what looked like, supplies. We drove for about an hour on quite a rugged road and eventually stopped in the wilderness. The driver and other man got out of the jeep to inspect the road in front. I got out to be nosey and to get some life back into my rear end. The road had come to a stop because it was flooded. It appears that the road should have taken us to the river. I could see in the not too far distance a fast-flowing river, Narayani River, the one that I had to cross to get to the island. The name of my destination was Island Jungle Resort, so of course, I would have to cross water to get to it. It never entered my mind before!

Suddenly, this little excursion was becoming real. Oh well, that is what I wanted, so go for it, girl. There was nothing else to do but wade through the flood water to get to the river. I was wearing a kurta surawal (tunic and baggy pants) which I thought would be appropriate wear for riding an elephant, unfortunately, not for wading thigh deep. The water seeped further up my baggy pants until they were totally wet. I was holding my bag above my head, just like one of those films where the main character has to wade across a river to get away from the bad men. Perhaps an exaggeration.

Eventually we reached the river. There had been a lot of rain that monsoon and much of the Terai had been flooded badly, and people had died. This was reality for them and here I was getting a kick out of the conditions. What did that make me? I shrugged off the thoughts. The river was extremely high and rapid. I looked around for a ferry to take us over to the island. Silly me, we weren't going to the Isle of Wight. Hitched onto the shore was a small dugout canoe. That was our transport. I wish I had learnt to swim.

Very cautiously I climbed into the canoe and took my seat. The water was literally six inches maximum from the top of the boat. A bit too close for comfort. The oarsman told me to keep my hands inside and not to dangle them in the water. The river was infested with crocodiles. I did wonder if my insurance would cover me for all eventualities, including being eaten or maimed by a crocodile. I was not comfortable near water, never have been. I blame my primary school swimming teacher who pushed me into Leek baths because I wouldn't jump in. She wouldn't get away with that nowadays. The only way across the river was by this canoe so I had to get on with it. The oarsman pushed the canoe away from the shore and off we set. The current was extraordinarily strong, and we were being washed down stream. But I had every faith in the oarsman. My mantra at times like this was, '*he doesn't want to die*' over and over again. He was very skilled and eventually we reached the other side of the river. I was in awe of his strength and fortitude. We alighted onto the island.

I had no pre-conceived ideas about what I was going to find. It certainly was not a sandy beach with swaying palm trees. And it was not roaming with giraffes and lions. Instead, it was literally a jungle of trees and bushes, with a clearing, a few yards in, for the resort. Interesting, I thought. I could hear squealing and lots of laughter. Water was being splashed and I could hear elephants trumpeting. In a gap in the trees, in a small inlet in the river, were three or four elephants. They were being 'washed' by half a dozen non-Nepali young people. From their accents as they shouted, they were European. They were sitting on the elephants' backs and the elephants were spraying them with water from their trunks. Everyone seemed to be having such a lot of fun. I would have loved to have joined in, but my fear of water prevented me from taking part in any aquatic activities. I was so envious of people who could just mess about in water.

I was greeted by the manager of the resort, a man a bit younger than me. I have decided to call him Prabin. He took me to the dining area and presented me with a bowl of noodle soup, chapatis and spiced tea. I was not a lover of tea, but I was growing to like the Nepali brew. He then led me to one of about four thatched open huts, where I ate my meal in peace. Prabin returned to explain my itinerary for the day. I would be going on an elephant ride to look for white one-horned rhino. I was really enthusiastic about the prospects of riding an elephant plus seeing a rhino. Must make sure I had a full battery in my camera.

It was about 3.30 pm when I was led down a path at the side of the main resort and taken to my transport for the afternoon. There stood a solitary elephant. I had never been in touching distance of one of these amazing animals and I felt quite emotional. I couldn't resist stroking him, although I am sure that he wouldn't have felt it through his thick skin. He was enormous, at least twice my height, with the tiniest of eyes. I named him Nelly, not very original but I felt he looked like a Nelly. Positioned alongside was a wooden platform which was accessed by a ladder. I climbed the ladder, stepped onto the platform which then allowed me to step onto a seating space, or howdah, on Nelly. It appears that these can seat up to eight people but as I was on my own, I could sit anywhere. I chose to be front facing with my feet on Nelly's neck. I didn't want to miss a thing.

We set off. A young man, a mahout, sat on Nelly's head and just in front of me, and guided Nelly with his feet and a stick. I must admit it was not the most comfortable ride I have ever had. Initially the movement of the swaying animal made me feel a bit motion sick. But that eventually wore off. The howdah was just wood which was a bit numbing, and my legs had to be straight in front of me and became stiff. However, the experience was incredible. Nelly plodded on slowly but surely along a beaten path, then when instructed would veer off into virgin foliage, ripping branches down with his trunk to create its own pathway. Occasionally, he would lift large branches that had fallen on the path and just move them to one side.

All I could hear were the sounds of insects and birds, and the swish, swishing of Nelly as we glanced through the trees. Sometimes we would walk down into little streams where he would have a drink. Sometimes we came to an abrupt stop while Nelly had a pee. Nothing would make him move until he had finished. He must have had a gigantic bladder to take so long. One time we stopped but no sound of peeing. The young man pointed to the ground and there was a tortoise, I am resisting calling it 'wild', which caused the elephant to freeze until it finished crawling past. It was not much bigger than a domestic tortoise and was certainly in no hurry. I had heard tales of elephants being frightened of tortoises and it was true.

I was at the same height as much of the canopy of the jungle so I could see the ground from a sort of birds-eye view. I saw a few monkey families high in the trees, a tree cobra, lots of deer, and at one time we had to stop because of a herd of wild boar raced in front of us. Strangely I did not see many insects, although my head did go through a few spider webs. One thing that fascinated me was the bark of the trees and how trees twisted around each other, especially at that height. They were a work of art.

We were 'on safari' for at least a couple of hours and it was starting to go dark. I had thoroughly enjoyed my time on Nelly. However, we had not seen any rhino. It was a shame, and it would have been nice to have seen one, but it was not the end of the world. I was grateful for what I had seen. We were greeted back at the elephant 'station' by Prabin who was disappointed that I had not seen a rhino.

"Tomorrow", he said. "You will definitely see one tomorrow", he insisted.

As we reached the main resort, I couldn't help noticing how quiet it was. I asked where the other visitors were, who I had seen earlier. They had left to go back to Pokhara. I was the only guest in the resort until tomorrow afternoon when a new group would arrive. Blimey, a whole jungle to myself!!

I spent the rest of that evening talking to Prabin and reading. I think he felt sorry for me because I was on my own, but I was honestly fine. His home was in the Terai, but several hours away. Unfortunately, his house had been swept away in the floods this season. His family was safe, but he was worried about where they were going to live. I was amazed at how matter of fact he sounded. I would have been in despair. I am sure he was, but it was part of his normal life, a life where you just have to get on with it as there is no option. I felt extremely humbled to be talking to such a man.

I did not read for long. The resort had no electricity at all and the light from a candle in the thatched hut was not very bright. I suppose that adds to the ambience of the experience. I was also getting eaten alive by the local mosquitoes. They are not supposed to be carriers of malaria as malaria had been eradicated in the Terai many years ago. However, their bites are unpleasant to say the least. I seem to attract them wherever I go. I was told that it was not because they liked my sweet diabetic blood but can't think of another reason. I had a busy day tomorrow, starting with an early morning elephant ride. So, I decided to get an early night. I had not been to my accommodation yet so was

65

interested to see what it was like. Fortunately, I had a torch with me which led me along a path to the room. Lanterns had been placed on the pathway which were really useful. The odd little reptile of sorts ran across the path. I did not look too closely in case they were not reptiles but mice or rats. However, at intervals were enormous snails, about the size of a coconut. They were incredible and seemed unreal. I was a little worried as the path skirted near to the edge of the river, which in the dark looked even more foreboding. I had visions of a crocodile jumping out of the water to devour me. But no, I was safe.

My accommodation was a small, thatched mud chalet. A lantern had been placed by the door for me to use inside. I checked my room for any unwanted visitors, but it was remarkably clear, except for some bright red centipede-type insects in the bathroom. Inspection done, I went to bed and slept reasonably well, only woken a couple of times with a hefty bang on the outside wall of my chalet. I was so tired; I just went back to sleep.

My early morning elephant ride was at about 7 am. I am not really a morning person, but I was up and raring to go. Prabin escorted me to the elephant station where I met up with Nelly again. Whilst the ride was similar in route to the day before, it was a quite different experience as everywhere was wet from the overnight rain. This made the atmosphere feel and smell so fresh. We set out again to find a rhino. I could feel the mahout's desperation to find one for me. Time and again we would break into virgin jungle, the man listening intently for any sound that showed we were near. No go. But he did point out some tiger tracks. Tigers are known to inhabit the jungle but are very rarely seen. After a couple of hours, he had to give up his search and we headed back. We were met by Prabin again who was really upset that I had not seen a rhino. I was genuinely fine about it. Animals are unpredictable. It was just one of those things. I had had my two elephant excursions that were my allowance in the trip itinerary. It was worth going to the resort for those. Despite the near unbearable heat and humidity, I was thoroughly enjoying my time there. After a late breakfast, Prabin collected me for a jungle walk and a stroll by the side of the river to see the crocodiles. Unfortunately, because of the flooding of the shores, we were unable to see the crocodiles bathing. Again, I was not too disappointed. I would, perhaps, come back another year when the weather conditions were better. We were gone for about one and a half hours. When back in the resort, we were joined by three groups of tourists: four from Russia, two from Wales, and another two from Eastern Europe. They were all young and boisterous. I no longer had the jungle to myself.

I went for a lie down. I had had a busy few hours, and the temperature drained me. I must have dozed off because I was awakened by a knocking on my door. "Didi, didi get up". I liked being called didi as it meant older sister. It was a less formal and friendly way of being addressed. Prabin was standing at my door. In a hushed voice he told me to follow him. It was all very furtive. Where was he taking me? He kept looking around to see if we were being followed.

We went behind the main resort buildings and there was Nelly. He was in, what I assume, was the elephant sleeping quarters. There were about four men standing with him and grinning. Aw, I am here to see where he sleeps. That's nice. No, Prabin, still in a whisper, said that I was to have another elephant ride because I hadn't seen the rhino. He said that it was breaking the rules of only two excursions, so he did not want the other visitors in the camp to know I had had three rides. They had already left for their first ride, so we were to hide from them. I was really touched by this gesture. How kind.

However, I could see a problem, a major one. There was no ladder and platform to get on Nelly. Nelly was instructed to crouch down. He was still much taller than me. How do I do this? Prabin patted Nelly halfway up his body. "Put your foot there, didi, and you will be pulled up". One of men had climbed up onto Nelly's back and was waiting for me. "There is no way I can get my leg up so high". I am sure that I had a similar conversation about a horse before. I tried really hard to do as I was told. But no go. A chair was brought for me to stand on and try to lift my leg above my head. Still no go. I admired Prabin's determination, but it was fruitless. The men had a conflab. They had a plan. I had visions of Nelly picking me up with this trunk and throwing me onto his back. Fortunately, that was not the plan.

Now you have to close your eyes and visualise this next bit. The chair was placed at the back of the elephant. I stood on the chair. Two men were now standing on Nelly, one was holding the tip of his tail, so his tail was looped. I followed the instruction to put my foot on the bend in Nelly's tail. And with that the men pulled Nelly's tail upward, and the rest of the men were pushing my backside, thus lifting me onto his back, very ungracefully. From there I crawled onto the howdah. Everyone cheered, quietly. You can open your eyes now.

We set off, yet again, on our intrepid mission to find a rhino. We wound our way through the jungle, sometimes on the beaten path and sometimes in virgin growth. We even went out of the thick of the jungle into an area of exceedingly high grass, all the time straining to see the elusive creature. At one point, the mahout stopped Nelly suddenly. He whistled loudly and received a whistle in return. With that he swung Nelly around and raced him at quite a fast pace through the trees, away from the direction of the whistle. This did not help my motion sickness and the feeling of numbness. "What is the matter?" I shouted. "Are we in danger?" No, it appears that another group of elephant riders were nearby, and we are supposed to be hiding from them. How exciting!

I was on Nelly for about three hours. It was obvious that the mahout had been told not to come back until I had seen a rhino. The sun was going down and my bladder was taking a beating. I thanked the driver and suggested that we went back to the resort. My suggestion went onto deaf ears. Suddenly, he sat up straight and looked to the right. He motioned to Nelly that we were to go through some fresh undergrowth, but slowly. A few seconds later, there in a small clearing was a baby rhino. It seemed unperturbed by our presence and carried on grazing. It was absolutely perfect. The miniature version of the creature we had been seeking was about 4' high, wearing it's armour plating and just one small horn protruding from its forehead. I know I have been saying that I was not disappointed not to see one before, but I felt extremely emotional at the sight of this beautiful beast. How could anyone want to kill these creatures just for the bit of ivory on their head? After a few minutes of staring in wonder at our find, the mahout turned Nelly and we went back to the resort. Mission accomplished!

Thankful, we went to the elephant station and platform, which saved me from having to unceremoniously slide off Nelly. We were met by Prabin. "Did you see it". "I did, I did, it was amazing. Thank you so much for giving me the opportunity". I was not sure who was more pleased about our success, me, Prabin, the mahoot, or Nelly. The rest of my stay in Chitwan could not top the pleasure I felt at that time. The rest of the visitors to the resort had finished their ride and were bathing the elephants, as yesterday. They were unaware of my clandestine 'third elephant ride'. Even when I spoke to them later on, and they told me that they had seen lots of rhinos, I did not declare my special one. There is something very smug about having a secret that no one else knows.

Natural World

Every country has its own flora and fauna, much of it dependant on climate and terrain. However, the extent to accessing animal life is often dependant on the culture of the country. In Britain we would only expect to see cows and sheep in fields belonging to farmers, and dogs with their owners in parks or in homes, whereas in countries like Nepal they can be seen anywhere they like to roam. During my earlier visits to Kathmandu, large packs of dogs of every sort could be seen on every street. Fortunately, they kept themselves to themselves most of the time. Even rats and mice, whilst not invited into homes, are not regarded as horrendous vermin as we do, or is it just me? Even insects are tolerated. Consequently, people like me who are used to animals being 'controlled' or more exotic/tropical animals being captive in zoos, are mesmerised and amazed by the natural world of Nepal.

Monkeys. I love monkeys. I watch all the TV programmes about monkeys. They are so engaging and funny. Their human features and mannerisms draw me to relate them to people I know - no names. I could watch them all day long playing and competing with each other. The baby ones are the cutest, finding their independence or clinging on to their mums. Monkeys are found in many places in Nepal, not just in the jungles but at religious temples and even on the urban streets. They tend to be macaque monkeys which are common throughout Asia. They are brown and grow to about two/three feet with a long tail. They are usually in large troupes with no fear of humans and generally people have little fear of them. I have only heard of a very few stories where monkeys have attacked or bitten people. Coming from Britain where monkeys are only seen on the TV or in zoos, I was thoroughly excited and entertained by monkeys playing within touching distance.

It is surreal to be standing at Pashupati Nath, the Hindu cremation temple, by the side of the Bagmati river, watching a solemn burning of someone's loved one and seeing monkeys irreverently chasing each other over the roofs or swinging from the statues or even cheekily pinching straw off the burning cremation pyre. Sometimes they would even swim and splash directly in front of the smouldering ghats. It seemed bizarre to be privy to such a poignant occasion yet a sublimely natural display of normality for the monkeys.

My first close-up encounter of a monkey was when I was invited to visit a young woman in a tiny room among the temples at Pashupati Nath. We climbed a loft ladder up to her first-floor room that she shared with her disabled son. As we walked over the floorboards with missing chunks, I noticed how dark the room was. No wonder, sitting on the window ledge and taking up the whole of the window space was a fully-grown adult monkey. It did not move for the whole duration of my visit. I felt obliged to say good-bye to the monkey and to thank him for his hospitality, as it seemed that he was the host, and we were his guests.

One of the places where monkeys are guaranteed to be seen is the Monkey temple or Swayambhu Nath, which stands on a hill in the NW of the Kathmandu valley. This is a stunning enormous white and gold stupa, topped with the 'all seeing eye of Buddha', surrounded by small temples, shrines, restaurants, shops and houses. Whilst it was built more than 1,500 years ago as a Buddhist temple, it is also revered by Hindus with many Hindu icons incorporated into the Buddhist features, showing the harmony of religions in this country. Brightly coloured Buddhist prayer flags by the thousands flutter from the stupa and other buildings, giving a feeling of permanent festival. It is no surprise that it is called the Monkey temple because of the hundreds of monkeys that inhabit the site. They can often be seen stealing edible offerings placed in the shrines or temples by worshippers. One of their main escapades is running over the roofs. On one visit I was sitting outside a little coffee shop when there was such a commotion. Three monkeys were chasing each other over the corrugated steel roofs and came flying over my head. I ducked down as initially I thought that it was debris falling. Once again, my next thought was whether my holiday insurance covered me for injury by flying monkeys!

The main entrance/exit to the stupa is via a very steep stone staircase of, reportedly, 375 steps. I must admit that the big sign that is placed at the start of the staircase that has a skull and crossbow, and the word 'DANGER' is not very reassuring as the first step down is taken. The staircase is lined with giant Buddhas and animal statues and vendors selling jewellery, tangkas, bells, thunderbolts, indeed anything that is classed as Nepalese and of religious significance, either from a tiny makeshift stall or carried, wrapped in a piece of cloth. These latter vendors are more difficult to get away from as they follow you whilst trying to use emotional blackmail for a sale. Even more difficult to escape from are the women with babies, begging for money for baby milk. I know everyone is trying to make a living and often a purchase from a tourist is the only way they and their families will eat that night, but the constant pleading is overwhelming at times and really one can only buy a finite number of souvenirs.

On one occasion I was with my grandson, Max, on his first visit to Nepal. I had promised him that there were hundreds of monkeys to see at the temple, but we were disappointed that there were very few. I was told that they were having their afternoon siesta. Oh well, we could go back another time. We plodded down the steps, me much slower. I have had several nasty falls in the country, so I was wary of stumbling. As we reached the halfway point, we saw dozens of monkeys clambering up the staircase. Siesta time was obviously over! Brilliant. My grandson was amazed at the spectacle they made. How can you not be?

We sat down on a little wall to take a breather and to watch the parade. It was really hot and humid, so I brought out of my bag a couple of bottles of coke for us. Max downed most of his in one go. I took a gulp of mine and screwed the top back on and sat with the bottle on my lap. Boy, did I need that! Suddenly, a large monkey strolled over to us. Wow, this will be a good photo opportunity, I thought. But he had not come to say 'hello'. He held out his hand and tried to grab my bottle of coke. I pulled it away and shouted, 'go away', or words to that effect. He looked at me with contempt and just snatched the bottle off me and sat down in front of us. He unscrewed the top, threw it down, and proceeded to gulp down my nearly full bottle of coke. He emptied it and threw it on the floor. Then with no politeness at all, snatched Max's bottle off him and drank what was left. There was no 'thank you' or 'nice to see you' just pure day-light robbery. He sauntered off to join his friends with not a care in the world. Max and I looked at each other in total amazement and then spent the rest of the journey to the bottom of the staircase laughing. I vowed to be more careful next time.

A few years later I was keen to show my husband the renowned Monkey temple. Rod had not been to Nepal before and so I was intent on showing him most of the beautiful and interesting attractions in Nepal, especially the monkeys. We had not been there long when I decided to have a sit down on a bench and just watch the monkeys perform. Rod, as most people who go there, was mesmerised by their playfulness.

In his pocket he had a bag of boiled sweets and asked if I wanted one. "Yes", I said, "but be careful that the monkeys do not see them". I was obviously wary after my 'coke fiasco'. Rod slipped his hand into his pocket and careful pulled out a sweet. It was well hidden in his clenched hand. Nonchalantly, he passed it to me. I received it in my clasped hand, confident that we had got away with it. Oh no, our undercover transaction had been spied. A large monkey bounded over to me; prised my fingers open one by one with his long slim fingers, took out the sweet, took off the paper and plonked the sweet into his mouth. He then proceeded to climb onto the seat next to me and crunch MY sweet. When he had swallowed it, he got off the seat and walked away as if to say, 'Job's done'. What can you do!!!!!

My most unexpected experience of monkeys was when I was staying in Ghandruk. I was in my room in the lodge where I was staying when I heard a commotion outside. People were shouting and running around. I ran out of my room to see what was going on. "Monkey, monkey" shouted one of the local boys. I had no idea that monkeys inhabit these high altitudes. It appears that they are regular visitors to the village and are unpopular for stealing and damaging the maize, the main crop grown here. The monkey was just behind the lodge in a maize field. I entered the spirit of the moment and joined in with the other people, chasing the monkey and squealing to frighten it away. It ran up the hillside, stopped, turned around and, I swear on my mother's grave, it looked at us with amusement and did the two-finger gesture. Not sure whether it was celebrating his get-away with the victory sign or just showing us total contempt. I think by the look on his face it was the latter.

I have come to the conclusion that the main 'game' for monkeys is theft, not slyly or sneakily, but down-right blatantly. That was shown in their robbery of the drinks, sweets and maize. Only a couple of years ago I visited an ashram, a monastic retreat in a national park on the outskirts of Kathmandu city. It was set on a hillside in a glorious location, surrounded by lush vegetation, bushes, flowers and trees. A Nepali friend had opened a restaurant in the ashram selling drinks and vegetarian food. It was at the entrance to the ashram, at the top of the hillside, with the accommodation and meeting room at the bottom of the hill. From the restaurant, that had large sliding windows, it was possible to see over the whole of the ashram and beyond. The view was stunning and bird life was incredible. There were all kinds of birds, various sizes and a multitude of colours, flying back and forth among the trees. There were spectacular bright red birds, vibrant green ones, and vivid yellow ones. I particularly liked the dazzling blue birds. Among the trees and particularly on the roof of the meeting room, was a troupe of monkeys. They do seem to have a fascination with roofs. The baby monkeys were using the sloping roof as a slide, slithering down and then running back and doing it all again. It was obvious that they were enjoying their time and it was a joy to watch. The restaurant served coffees and tea from behind a modern counter- impeccably clean and practical. The tables were the same but, unlike other restaurants I had been in, there were no condiments on the table, salt/pepper pots, sugar bowls etc., I soon found out why.

As I sat by the window, watching the entertainment, a large monkey jumped in through the open window, strolled past me and my friend, went behind the counter as if he knew where he was going, and with no conscience at all, picked up a sugar bowl with loose sugar in it, balanced it in the palm of his hand and walked out. He stopped and perched on the windowsill, looked directly at us as if he were saying, "Don't even think about stopping me. It is my right to have this sugar". And climbed out of the window to join his friends. I was aghast, the nerve of him. My friend was unperturbed. He claimed that that happened all the time and that was why there was nothing on the tables. I rest my case.

The freedom offered to animal life in Nepal does not cease to fascinate me, especially the cows and buffalo that are allowed to roam wherever they want. Less so now, but on my earlier visits to Nepal I did not tire of seeing cows and buffalo strolling in the urban streets, even in the tourist areas. The buffalo are enormous with huge, curled horns. I assume they are owned by someone somewhere. Even now, it was not uncommon to see half a dozen cows or buffalo lying curled up in the middle of a main road and fast asleep. All traffic has to skirt around them. Cows are sacred in Hindu culture so any damage to them could result in a hefty fine or even imprisonment. I think that buffalo command the space just by their size. So just imagine your local ring-road or high street jammed full of cars, motorbikes, buses, lorries and rickshaws at peak time and being greeted by a buffalo walking towards you or just having a rest on the middle white line. I have taken so many photos of these creatures and I am sure I will continue to do so.

Some people would think that they meander in dangerous places because they are stupid. Well trust me, they are not. One day I was walking along the ring-road when the heavens opened. It was monsoon time and when it rained it came down like stair rods. I was only wearing flip flops, so my feet kept slipping out of them. I eventually reached a covered bus shelter. Great, and there were not too many people in it. My personal space did not last too long. In strolled a black cow, claiming its protection from the rain. It's enormous torso and head nearly filled the shelter. All the people moved out, but I stood my ground. I was here first. Chloe the cow (I named her) and I had an incredibly special five minutes until the rain stopped and we both moved on. Now tell me cows are stupid.

My affection for furry things does not stretch to rats and mice. I am really frightened of rats. People tell me that they do not really jump and bite your throat. But I have no intention of proving it. I have seen quite a few rats during my time in Nepal. Many are dead in the road. I can cope with that. But I have seen them scurrying in restaurant court yards. Some are the size of cats. OK I am exaggerating a bit. But they are big. I always put my feet up on a plinth under the table whenever I eat out. A rat ran over my foot in Bangkok, and I certainly do not want a repeat performance. Whenever I choose a hotel in Nepal it must fit certain criteria, especially as I am usually a lone traveller. It must be safe, clean, reasonably priced as I go on a shoestring, own bathroom, and no rats. After years of experience, I always insist on not having a ground floor bedroom to lessen the chance of rats sneaking under the door. I should have expanded my criteria to a room that is not a single storey.

Many of my visits took me to Pokhara, a town about 125 miles from Kathmandu. This a scenic town set by the largest lake in Nepal, the Phewa Tal, which reflects the spectacular Annapurna and Fishtail mountains. Many tourists flock there to rest and prepare themselves for trekking the mountains. The main road is full of shops aimed at the tourists and open fronted restaurants with music by Eric Clapton and Bob Marley playing out onto the streets. Everywhere is so laid back, especially after the chaos and hectic environment of Kathmandu. Indeed, I describe Pokhara as the place where 'I'll do it tomorrow as I can't be bothered to do it today'. A real hippy town.

I have stayed in a range of hotels there and have always tried to keep to my criteria. One of my visits to Pokhara saw me going back to a hotel that I have stayed in before. I was pleased with my accommodation last time so 'better the devil you know....'. I arrived late afternoon and they were nearly booked up. However, they did have a room at the back of the hotel – a single storey, ground floor room. Yikes, I pleaded with the manager for a first-floor room. Sorry, not until tomorrow. "It is a lovely room" he said. Reluctantly, I accepted the room and was shown to it. It ticked most of the boxes. It was quite small but looked clean enough. The roof was corrugated iron sheets, which I am not too keen on as they make hell of a din when it rains. The ceiling was straw rafters.

I lay on my bed to veg out for a few minutes before I went to look for a meal. Suddenly I heard the patter of tiny feet. They were coming from the rafters above my bed. I could also see something moving but wasn't able to make it out. I literally jumped off the bed and heard them again. There must be rats in the ceiling. I raced over to the office to tell the manager.

"I have rats in my ceiling".

"How do you know?"

"I heard them scurrying around".

"No madam they are birds on the roof".

"No, they are definitely rats. Birds hop, rats scurry. I know the difference between a bird and a rat. I want another room".

"Sorry madam but we don't have one".

I was in a quandary. It was starting to get dark; I was hungry, and I could not face looking for another hotel.

"Ok, I give in", I said. "I am going for a meal and when I get back if there is any evidence at all of rats in my room I will scream and scream until you find me another room. I don't care what time it is and if I wake up the whole of the hotel and Pokhara". And off I stropped.

I was gone for about two hours. I was so tired. I had travelled to Pokhara from Kathmandu on a bus which took 9 hours. I opened my door, put on the light and there, on my clean white pillow were rat droppings. There was at least a dozen. I froze. They must have dropped from the rafters. I stormed out and found the manager.

"I have got rat droppings on my pillow".

"No, Madam perhaps they are bird droppings".

"No, they are rat droppings. I know the difference between rat droppings and bird shit. I want a new room now, this second or I will start to scream and believe me I am loud". I took a deep breath. He could see I meant business. "Hang on, I will find you a room".

Low and behold, within 5 minutes he came back with keys to another room which was on the first floor, just like magic. He even helped me to move my stuff to the new room and when he looked at my pillow agreed that they were rat droppings. I did not ask where he had miraculously found my new room. In fact, I didn't care.

Now mice are a different ball game. I am not so much frightened of mice; I just don't like when they scurry around. They seem to pop out from anywhere. They can hide in the smallest of places, just waiting to crawl up your legs and give you horrible diseases. I'm not sure where my dislike of mice comes from as I had pet mice as a child. Not being discriminatory, but they were white ones which was different. And I suppose a single mouse isn't too scary. However, I did have an experience that would possibly make anyone shudder slightly.

A friend, Jean, and I had been taken to a village outside the Kathmandu valley, just a mere five hours drive away, where it was possible to see a clear panoramic view of the Himalayas. Unfortunately, as it was monsoon season, we did not get the view we had hoped for. In fact, we couldn't see much more than a few feet away because of the clouds. I was not surprised as I always go to Nepal in this season and had had several disappointing non-views of the mountains. But it would have been nice for Jean to see them.

This place had been chosen by a Nepali friend and he had chosen the hotel where we were to stay for one night. In fact, it was the only hotel in the village, but it seemed to be a good standard. The hotel manager was pleased to see us as we were the only guests. We were shown to a beautiful twin room with a balcony. The beds were big with thick mattresses. I am not one to complain but the mattress in my room in Kathmandu was about one inch thick, great if you have a bad back and want a firm mattress, but not so good if you don't arrive with a bad back, as a couple of nights of that, you get a bad back. So, this mattress was luxury.

We had a wander around the village and had supper of dahl bhat in the 'not so plush' dining room. People tend to go to bed early in the rural areas, so we retired to our room. After playing cards and chatting for ages, as women do, we bedded down. I turned off the bedside lights. The bed was so lush, and I felt myself becoming drowsy. Peace!!! Suddenly I heard rustling coming from the dressing table.

Jean said, "Did you hear that?". "Yes, you put the light on. I daren't see what it is". "No, you". We decided to do it together. The lights went on and what we saw was incredible. It was like a bad dream because it was so unreal. Without exaggerating, there must have been at least twenty mice running from under a gap at the base of the balcony door, along the wall, up onto the dressing table and into my rucksack. I had a bag of sweets in it in case I had a hypo (I'm diabetic). I could hear them munching on the paper, then they came out of the bag and ran along the rest of the dressing table and down the back. I screamed. My friend was amazed but didn't seem too horrified, unlike me. She was a country-girl so was not fazed and was somewhat irritated by my 'over' reaction. My Nepali friend came running to the room to save us but by then the mice had disappeared. He plugged the hole in the balcony door and left.

Needless to say, I didn't sleep much that night. The next morning, we went for breakfast in the 'not so plush' dining room. I had two boiled eggs and a slice of 'toast', after which we went to see the manager to report what had gone on that night. He laughed, "We get them everywhere. They are only field mice, and we live in the countryside, so they are always coming inside. We get many in the kitchen". That was not what we wanted to hear, especially as we had just finished breakfast. It was my friend's turn to be horrified. We asked for a discount on our room bill, but he said that mice were part of rural life and so no discount.

Getting back to rats. In all truth, I have not actually seen the offending rats that have tested me. I did not see the rats that drove me out of my room in Pokhara and I did not see the rats in my room that I had taken on my journey to Ghandruk. But I knew they were there. I had walked up to Ghandruk three times during my early visits to Nepal. The track is one of the most popular for trekkers to the country. The route to Ghandruk from Naya Pul, where the road finished and on foot was the only form of travel, has been described in the travel guides as a staircase as it is so steep and takes a normal trekker about four hours to climb. It took me at least nine hours. As you will gather from my earlier accounts, I do not like walking uphill. I am not built for trekking and I certainly would not describe my journeys as trekking. Trekking is supposed to be enjoyable. I walked/struggled/crawled up. It was not enjoyable by any stretch of the imagination. I think you get the idea!

Anyway, on my fourth planned journey to Ghandruk I decided that I would take it steady and stop to enjoy the stunning views of the mountains, the forests, rivers, waterfalls and vegetation. I would do the trip in two days and stop at one of the many guest houses overnight. So, I set off up the 'staircase'. My porter had gone ahead to Ghandruk with my bags so I could amble up in my own time. I stopped every now and then to take in the views but really to get my breath back. This is the life!

I knew that there would be no trouble getting accommodation for the night as it was not trekking season, and so few trekkers needing accommodation. So, I just needed to study the various advertising signs *en route* of guest houses/lodges. At the bottom of a particularly steep part of the trail was a sign for a guest house which was extremely enticing. '......Guest House, beautiful views, hot and cold running water, homemade tasty food, clean individual rooms, clean sheets, only 5 minutes away'. Just what I wanted. It would set me up for the next day. I was so slow that by the time I reached my accommodation it was starting to go dark, and it certainly took longer than 5 minutes.

The moment I arrived at the guest house I realised that I had made a mistake in asking the manager for a room. Anyway, to cut a long story short, I was eventually shown to my room. There was no electricity in the guest house, it had not reached that part of the Himalayas yet. My light came from a very short candle which was held up by the manager's son, who escorted me to my room by climbing a loft ladder. The room was basic with only a bed. The son said "Nice?" I gulped. The bed was covered in a sheet that had seen better days and the pillowcase was black with grime. "Yes, thank you" I said, doing the British thing by being polite.

Suddenly, in the corner of my eye I saw something move on the wall. It was the biggest spider I had ever seen. It was bigger than the size of my hand. As calmly as I could I said, "Please would you remove that spider". I do not mind spiders when I can see them, but as I would have no light, I wanted it gone. The son tried to reassure me, by telling me that it is not poisonous so it would be ok. I told him in no uncertain terms that I was fussy who I share my bed with and a spider that size was not getting the chance. He removed it.

The floor in my room was planks of wood on straw rafters. I could see through the planks into the owners' private room. The window had no glass, just shutters that had been left open. Whilst it is not as humid in the hills as in the city, it was still warm, so I left the shutters open. I needed the toilet. I also could have done with a wash. I'm posh like that! I climbed down the ladder to seek out a bathroom. I asked the owner of the guest house if I could have a shower. He looked shocked and said, "But you have to book it". I said, "Why, I am the only person here". To which he replied, "But I have to put the kettle on". With that I gave up and asked where the washing facilities were. I was shown a hosepipe, literally on the trail. I suppose that I was lucky to have that. I decided that *eau de BO* wasn't too bad after all.

I was directed to the toilet. The only path to the toilet was through the buffalo shelter. The buffalo were not amused at my presence and bellowed loudly. The son was just sweeping the toilet out and throwing a bucket of water in the hut to clean it. This seemed to make no difference to the cleanliness of the facility, long-legged spiders were hovering about my head. It was a pit latrine, which are common in Nepal and many other countries. Indeed, I have read articles that claim that these squatting technics are much better for your health than Western style ones. Personally, I find them somewhat difficult after a day's walking, plus having to watch out for marauding insects.

Back I went to my room, past the buffalo and up the ladder. The unhygienic bed was not particularly inviting but I was so tired by now. I decided to sleep fully clothed, even in my hiking boots, so that I could make a quick getaway in the morning. I lay on the bed listening to the family below and slowly closing my eyes. I had blown out the candle in order to save it for emergencies. I literally had half an inch left.

Suddenly, I heard crunching. I had put a carrier bag on the windowsill. I did not want to leave it on the floor in case something crawled into it. Instead, something was gnawing its way through it. It sounded bigger than a mouse and I believe that it was a rat or two. Or was it just me being dramatic? I closed my eyes and hoped it would stop. No, it was still crunching. I knew that if I lit my candle and actually saw that it was a rat, I would not be able to help but scream. I didn't want to wake the family and, to be truthful, I was embarrassed as they would only laugh at my fear. I just lay on my bed and waited for the unwelcome visitor to stop. It seemed like a lifetime. I spent the rest of night wide awake waiting for the sun to rise so that I could make a getaway, which I did.

You will have gathered by now that I am not the bravest person when it comes to unwelcome guests of the non-humankind. Neither am I the most knowledgeable about their habits. Indeed, at times I have been guilty of wrongly identifying animals, or even being ignorant of a species or two, especially during my early visits. I must admit that I was pretty naïve about the amount of wildlife I would be encountering. When I was planning my first trip to Nepal that side of things never crossed my mind, except for mosquitoes, as I did not relish the idea of contracting malaria. In fact, my family and friends, especially my husband, were more concerned about potential insects and spiders than I was. I think they had watched too much of African Queen.

On my first visit to Nepal, I stayed in a hotel in Pokhara for a couple of days before venturing up to Ghandruk. The hotel was very posh and somewhat out of my price range (I had not chosen it, but I did have to pay for it). The hotel consisted of small, thatched chalets. Pretty, impeccably clean and quiet.

I was extremely nervous about the impending journey up to Ghandruk so found it difficult to get off to sleep. It was July, Pokhara is much warmer than Kathmandu, and more humid, a tropical climate, which is accentuated during the monsoon season. Personally, I find the atmosphere oppressive, especially at night. Another reason why I couldn't sleep. I lay awake listening to the high shrill noises from outside. I was told that they come from insects that live in the surrounding trees that make the noise by rubbing their legs together. I don't know what they are called but they are loud.

I turned over in bed. There was a telephone on my bedside cabinet. I blinked. It couldn't be. I blinked again. It was. On the phone was the silhouette of a large insect. I could just make it out in the half light. I stayed calm and put the light on. The insect was a bright green praying manta which was the length of the telephone receiver. Strangely, I wasn't frightened of this. It was stunning, the colour, the shape and the size. In a flash it had jumped off the phone and onto the floor. It ran under my bed and vanished. I spent a while looking for it but no sign whatsoever. I was unnerved by its disappearance but at the same time excited to have seen something that I had only seen in books before. And, yes, another reason why I could not sleep. I had no chance. Too much mental stimulation.

The following day was my journey to Ghandruk, suffice to say I was exhausted by the time I arrived. I was shown to my accommodation for the next two weeks. It was a small room, basic but very clean, with a little vase of flowers on the bedside cabinet. It was so much better than my initial offer of the cow shed. Don't ask. As in most buildings in the area, there were no glass windows, just shutters. Mine had been left open for my arrival, so I left them. It turned dark early, so I had supper and retired to my room. We were lucky in Ghandruk, electricity had arrived a couple of years before, so I had put on a light bulb which lit my room well. I spent a while writing up my diary and getting ready for bed. It was so good to take off my thick wet socks and heavy hiking boots. I then closed the shutters and dropped onto the bed.

Remarkably, I dropped off to sleep quite soon but woke after a couple of hours. I sleep on my stomach and was aware that there was something moving on my back. In my hazy state, I flicked it off and it flew across the room. I grabbed my torch to see what it was. It was a flat brown insect, about 5-6 inches long, which I found out later was a cockroach. I also found out later that they are attracted to light and would have come into my room before I closed my shutters. I should have closed them before it went dark. I appeased myself that it was my fault that the cockroach had visited me, so I would be more careful next time. But still shudder when I think of it.

That same night after the cockroach episode, I managed to get back to sleep for a couple more hours. It was the first morning there and so I was daydreaming of what the day would hold for me. I moved my foot and felt a damp patch on the sheets. I looked down and there was patch of blood, about the size of small side plate on my crisp white sheet. Blood was coming from my big toe. Oh, dear me, I thought, I must have clipped the flesh when I cut my toenails before my journey. I looked at the bloody mess again and in the thick of it was a big fat black slug thing. Yuk. How did it get there? I picked it up and threw it into my upturned open umbrella and threw them both out of the door onto the path. I got dressed and went outside. There were some trekkers (real, proper trekkers) walking past my room. I asked them what was still sliming in my umbrella. "Gee", they were American, "that leech sure had a good feast last night". I recalled that on my way to Ghandruk, it was raining and during one of my many stops I had pulled off my socks to wring them out and I had a couple of little thread sized leeches on my feet which dropped off easily. One of the little buggers must have stayed in my sock and waited to have a midnight banquet. I couldn't believe that leeches that start off so small and insignificant can suck so much blood to become so voluminous. Unfortunately, during my consequential trips to Ghandruk I have physically supported and kept alive many leeches.

I must admit that on my first visit to Nepal I was not prepared for the terrain and what was to greet me there. I was reasonably fit but not a great walker. I believed that I would be fine. Despite my apparent cockiness, it was plain to see that I was not prepared for my first journey up to Ghandruk. My fitness was only on the flat but not appropriate enough for walking up and up hills. I did frighten one of my walking companions, a local woman, when I just sat down on the trail and said I was waiting for a taxi. She said, "No taxi, no road" to which I replied, "Well I am going to wait until they build one". Needless to say, I had to carry on. Indeed, my inner child came out of me yet again.

Anyway, before my second trip up to Ghandruk the following year I got into training. I felt that I was much fitter and so set off on the walk up to the village feeling confident. All was going well, then the heavens opened. We had only gone halfway and took refuge in a tea house until it stopped raining. Well, it didn't. My porter and I waited and waited but no reprieve. So, we set off again, me with my pink brolly – very colonial.

I instructed my porter to go ahead. We had a routine. He would walk on with my bags for about twenty minutes, and I would catch him up. It would give him a rest and he did not witness me gasping for breath and in pain whilst walking up the steep staircase as the more we climbed. My regained fitness had been washed away in the rain. Each time I stopped I sat on a chautara, a stone platform, to rest. Each time my porter would tell me not to, but I would ignore him. I knew better and my inner child had taken possession of me. I was constantly finding small leeches on my arms and legs. The little devils perch on the vegetation and hook onto any unsuspecting idiot who sits on walls. I was wearing a short sleeve t-shirt and long skirt. The long skirt enabled toileting easier than dragging trousers on the floor. But they also allowed the leeches to latch onto my legs. Fortunately, they did not stay on me for too long, just enough to puncture my skin and take a quick mouthful. I could cope with that.

This plan worked for a while then I lost my porter. I thought there was only one track to the village so where could he have gone? In fact, where had the track gone? The sun was going down, it was still raining, and I became increasingly worried. I did not want the headlines in the British newspapers to be 'English grandmother lost in the Himalayas'. I staggered past a small house and knocked on the door. A young girl came out. Using my poor communication skills, I managed to ask, "Where is the track to Ghandruk?" She pointed to a stream running down the hillside. "Ghandruk", she said. The track had turned into a stream and that is what I had to walk up. I was truly becoming Indiana Jones. I splashed up the steam. I was drenched already, so filling my boots with water was a minor problem. Suddenly, my porter came running down the hill. I am not sure who was happier to see who.

He took me to a tea house to recuperate. It was getting darker and still raining. Directly in front of us was the track we were to walk along. However, there was an active landslide that was falling onto the track. It had been rumbling for a few days. My porter did not want to risk walking through it. Our only hope was to climb up and over the top of the landslide and through the jungle. It would add at least an hour onto our journey, but it looked as if I had no choice. We climbed up and up the hillside. There was no beaten track, so it was just mud and grass. I kept stumbling and falling into the vegetation. This meant that I was prey to the leeches. This time they were eager to attach themselves to my arms, hands and between my fingers. My porter took it upon himself to save me from being sucked alive and pinch the leeches off my skin one after another, after another. Dozens. He, fortunately, was adept at pulling them off as I didn't relish them being burnt off with a cigarette or match as had been advised in survival books. We walked through the jungle, it was pitch dark by then and I was staggering like a drunkard. The leeches just kept coming and my porter kept saving me. At last, there was light. We had reached Ghandruk, and I was still alive.

My Nepalese friend, Jagan, who owned the lodge where I was staying, led me carefully to my room and put the light on. I was soaked right through. My clothes, in particular my skirt, were covered in leeches. Fortunately, the lodge had a shared shower and a Western style toilet which is useful when you have been trekking. Jagan guided me to the shower room, turned on the shower and left me to it. I took off my T-shirt and my skirt and let out a scream. My body was covered in black juicy leeches, dozens of them. I even had them in my bra and in my pants. It was like a horror film. I screamed again and my porter ran in to save my life. He took one look at my half naked body, covered his mouth and ran out of the shower room. It was like a British farce.

I can laugh about it now, but not then. Jagan came to my rescue. Between us we managed to extract the leeches. Leeches do not hurt but leave a puncture wound which bleeds profusely. The ones on my legs wouldn't stop bleeding, so Jagan carefully placed small pieces of pink toilet roll on the wounds to stem the flow of blood. That is what you call a true friend. I had gone to Ghandruk to conduct research, in a professional capacity. I was expecting to interview leaders and local people. But by the morning the whole of the village knew of my disastrous journey and even more so my pathetic performance. I suppose it 'broke the ice' and gave people something to laugh about.

I presumed that that was the end of my association with leeches, but no. The monsoon rains were persistent that year, so most of my visiting and wandering around the village was done in the rain. I had to get used to the leeches attaching themselves to my legs. What I did object to was when they slurped my face and tried to burrow into my ears. Not nice! One species of creepy-crawly that I do like very much is the butterfly, especially those found in Nepal, where there is an abundance of them. They are everywhere, and all colours and sizes. I am not sure how people get beautiful photos of them because as soon as I get my camera out, they are gone. Pokhara seems to have a larger range, possibly because it is tropical. After only seeing a few varieties in the UK, watching dozens of different sorts in Nepal is a real treat. There is a specific spot on the trail to Ghandruk where, without exaggeration, there were hundreds of small bright yellow butterflies fluttering *en masse*. I had to flail my arms about to disperse them so that I could carry on walking. Absolutely stunning.

One of my favourite butterflies is found in the urban and rural areas. They are as big as my hand and are black/very dark blue with sky blue on their wings. Unlike the other butterfly sorts, they do not seem to be as nervy and don't fly off as quickly. Or perhaps I have learnt to be more stealth-like over the years. This butterfly seems to be quite common in Ghandruk. The vegetation is lush, and the air is clean, ideal for butterflies. On my first visit to Ghandruk, I seem to have learnt a lot on that visit, I had been able to forge a friendship with one of the large black butterflies. I actually managed to gently stroke its wing and talk to it as it settled near to me. I felt like a cross between David Attenborough and Dr Doolittle. What a privilege to be in this amazing environment and to be at one with a butterfly! Ok, I was getting carried away. It was only one caress, but it meant a lot to me.

That night I went to the small dining room at the lodge where I was staying and had my supper of momos, sort of spicey dumplings. It had gone dark and so I decided to have an early night. As I came out of the dining room into the open courtyard, something caught my eye. I turned and looked at the window of the dining room. Hanging from it were a few ears of corn and about four of these black butterflies with their wings folded. I was thrilled, especially as I thought that perhaps one was 'my' earlier acquaintance. With no hesitation I put my finger out to stroke one of them. And then quickly withdrew it. The 'butterflies' had teeth and were hanging upside down. They were bats. OMG bats!!!!! I ran to my room which was across the courtyard, with my shawl covering my head. I knew about bats and how they fly onto your head and get tangled in your hair and bite your head. I was taking no chances.

Matters of Health

Alexandra Pope (1709) said that 'a little knowledge is a dangerous thing', whilst Thomas Gray (1768) said 'that ignorance is bliss'. I think that these two sayings are applicable to me, especially when it comes to matters of health. Sometimes it is better not to know too much about illness or the repercussions, especially where local conditions are not adequate or as wished. It could frighten you to a heart attack. I have spent many years lecturing in a university on health and development in developing countries. However, I do not claim to be an expert on health issues, far from it, but over my years of researching, travelling and just existing I have picked up quite a bit of information about things that can go wrong with the human body. In fact, I have always had a fascination for that sort of thing. I can remember as a young child watching 'Your life in their hands' where very graphic footage of open surgery was shown on the TV. I was mesmerised, although I am not sure if I would have felt the same if the TV was in full colour and not black and white.

Saying that, I do have a phobia about needles. I can remember fainting when I was five years old when we all had to have a vaccination at school. After that, whenever we had a letter sent home for our parents to give permission for later vaccinations, I tore it up. I was not going to be put through that again. Indeed, when I was about 13 years old, I fainted when my friend had her TB jab at school. I didn't even see it. Ironically, to go to Nepal, I had to have an armful of jabs, including the missed childhood ones and lots of others that I had previously escaped from. What is more, my daughter had to have masses of injections, blood tests and transfusions as part of her treatment, which I had to sit through and be 'brave' for her sake. I did have to walk out of the room when the doctors tried to take blood from her groin. And now, as a penance for my former indiscretions, I have to inject myself twice daily because of diabetes.

The choice of study for my doctorate was guided by my fascination for all things to do with health. My research into the social aspects of leprosy took me to a new level of exploration of health issues. I interviewed more than 150 people affected by the disease and heard stories of human behaviours that I will remember for always. I was told of tremendous bravery and sacrifice of people affected by leprosy and their families, and of people being treated like animals with verbal and physical cruelty, stigmatisation and banishment from their own home and villages.

Whilst, hopefully, teaching me some lessons in humanity and compassion towards others, the study did grant me a PhD, which enabled me to call myself 'Doctor'. Strangely, whilst being proud of my accomplishment and hopefully my contribution to the knowledge of this disease, the title 'doctor' always seemed to be inappropriate for me to use. For me, it seemed to disrespect 'real doctors'. I know that is stupid. I really have earned my title. And I don't want to take the importance of it away for other 'doctors', but that is my mindset. However, I must admit that I do use it to my advantage sometimes, such as when I go to see the bank manager, want to make a complaint or need to visit someone important in Nepal. Indeed, when I was studying for my undergraduate degree, I was called Master in Nepal, and now I am a doctor I am called Professor. Who is not wanting to be called that? My rise in status really does carry a lot of credence.

One such incident was when I was in a place called Jomson. Jomson is high in the Himalayas, on the Annapurna trail. The only way of getting there was at least a five-day trek or a flight from Pokhara. My friend, Jagan, used to work there and wanted to show me the village. Naturally, we decided to fly to Jomson. I would have walked there but we only had a couple of days to do it in. (I am lying of, course). Only small aircraft fly to Jomson, one reason being that the runway is noticeably short, just 2,500 feet with a sheer drop at the end, and the plane has to access the village by flying along the Kali Gandaki Gorge with mountains close on either side. Because of the location between the mountains, plus strong winds later in the day, flights tend to stop to and from Pokhara after 11am, to prevent them from being flung against the rocks. The flight is only about twenty minutes long and, when travelling this way, I must admit I am relieved when I see a Buddhist monk sitting near to me. It is also a comfort to see in the cockpit effigies of Hindu gods, Buddha, virgin Mary, Jesus, and Sai Baba. I have also been known to repeat a mantra under my breath, 'the pilot does not want to die'.

Jomson was hugely different from other villages I had visited in Nepal. It was very barren; brown was the dominant colour with a lunar landscape. In fact, Sting's 'Walking on the Moon' was said to have been influenced by his visit to Jomson. The village, back then, was just one road lined with restaurants, tea houses and small hotels. It was on the main trail to Muktinath, a religious location revered by both Buddhists and Hindus. We stayed in the village for two nights. I did have a touch of altitude sickness throughout my stay. It was only 9,000 feet but I did feel nauseas, headachy, and a bit spaced out. Some people would say that is normal for me! At the time, I did not know that was altitude sickness but recognised it when I went to Tibet a few years later and got a severe form of it.

In the village there appeared to be just one telephone line that went along the road. I had an interest in alternative medicine and had heard that there was an herbalist down the road. I phoned him from my hotel reception. "Hello, this is Dr Janet Jones. I was wondering if I could come and talk to you about your traditional medical methods?" An appointment was agreed, and I put the phone down. As I turned around, there was a young English woman waiting to talk to me. She looked in discomfort. "Hello, Dr Jones, I was hoping that you can help me. I have the most awful constipation." I was totally thrown. "Ey duck", I said. "I'm not that sort of a doctor. But I usually take Ex-lax". I could tell she was disappointed but what could I do? She had had to break off from trekking because she felt so bad. I saw her walking around Kathmandu the following week. She had had to go to hospital to be 'unblocked'. Poor thing.

Indeed, the title 'Doctor' is not needed in some cases to attract people needing health advice. Just being a Westerner can be enough. During one of my earlier visits to Ghandruk, I was asked for guidance totally out of my comfort zone. I was at the lodge where I was staying when a local woman came up to me. She was obviously in pain and showed me her arm. It was very swollen and red. Using my extremely poor communication skills, I asked how she had got the injury. "Fallen?" And pretended to fall. "No", she said. "Insect bite?" And made the sound of a mosquito and pinched my skin. "No". Instead, she hissed and imitated a bite to her arm. She had been bit by a snake. Flaming Nora! I had not thought of that one. What to do? I had seen western films where people like John Wayne would suck out snake venom or use a knife to open the wound to let the poison out, but I didn't fancy either of those. Brilliant, Jagan arrived. "Help, this woman has a snake bite. What can we do?" I sounded desperate. Calmly Jagan said, "She needs to go to the health centre, but it is closed today. She will have to come back tomorrow". With that, the woman lit up a cigarette, shrugged her shoulders and walked away. I often wondered how she got on.

On a personal note, I have had my fair share of ailments during my stays in Nepal. As many visitors to countries like Nepal have found out the hard way, gastro-enteric problems or stomach bugs are common occurrences. Frequently, conversations can be heard about how many times someone has 'been' today, or advice on what to eat/drink to stop 'going'. I have had stomach problems, including dysentery, many times. I think that 'knowledge' is important to prevent or minimise the episodes. However, sometimes ignorance is bliss when it comes to knowing what is going on inside the body. The thought of intestinal worms wriggling inside the body freaks me out. I once had giardiasis, a particularly unpleasant condition, where tiny worm-type things latch onto the walls of the intestines. I made a mistake of looking the condition up in a book with photographs. Nightmarish. I suggest you do not do the same. I won't go through the ins and outs of my bowel habits when in Nepal, suffice to say that I became extremely knowledgeable about the range of 'latrines' on offer, particularly public ones.

Before embarking on my travels, I always make an appointment with the dentist for a thorough check up. It is high on my 'to do' list. I had a particularly nasty experience during one of my early trips to Nepal which has made me extra cautious about having healthy teeth. I had been in Ghandruk for a few days and settling in nicely when I woke up with raging toothache. It was a tooth that had been problematic for quite a while. The root was exceptionally long and growing in a difficult direction. My dentist had suggested that it be left alone while it was not bothering me as any treatment could be very invasive and awkward. I had this conversation in mind when I prowled around my room wishing the pain to go away. In a moment of madness, I decided to look up in the Lonely Planet Guide about dentists in Nepal. This is another incidence where ignorance is bliss. In the guidebook, it said, 'Dentist – just hope you never have to use one.' Did that make me feel better, now that I knew that? Definitely not. The pain seemed to intensify.

What I did know was that cloves could help. Unfortunately, in my first aid kit there were none. I also had heard that a crushed soluble aspirin pushed on the tooth could help or an aspirin gargle. Guess what? I had none. I had Brufen for pain, which I took. It dulled the pain slightly for only a short while. I started to get very frightened about my predicament. There was no way that I was allowing an unknown dentist to take my tooth out. My mind went back to a road on the way to Indra Chowk in Kathmandu where several dentists were holding surgeries. Many of them were just inside the doorways or closed off by a flimsy curtain. In the windows were sets of or individual teeth that you could choose from. If all else failed on the same road, there was a shrine to the God of Toothache, which was a place where people with toothache could hammer in a coin and the toothache would go. I was not comforted by these images.

I decided that the only thing to do was to visit the doctor at the health post in Ghandruk and ask for some soluble aspirin or an antibiotic. The health post was a short walk away and a tremendous addition to the village, where only a few years ago there was no formal healthcare except for the local jhakri, lama or shaman. The doctor was not at the health post that day, but I explained my pain to an assistant. "Brufen" she said. "No, not for toothache", I replied. "Yes, Brufen", she insisted. "Pain will go". With that she walked away from me. I did have Brufen in my first aid kit and had already taken some but if the assistant insisted that that would help, I would persevere. I did, through that day and the night. But I was not getting any real relief. I went back down to the health post to try and catch the doctor. He was not there again. I asked the assistant for some antibiotics. "Sorry, they have run out. There will not be another delivery until one month". "Then please, let me have some soluble aspirin". I pleaded. "No, Brufen" and with that she took a strip of the tablets off a shelf and gave them to me. I was hitting a brick wall. I went back to my room, totally despondent.

Later that evening, two trekkers arrived at the lodge. I told them about my toothache and my failure to get some aspirin from the health post. One of the trekkers had some soluble aspirin and gave me what he had left. There were only about four but were received very gratefully. I immediately gargled with one and then I bit into another, pushing it against my offending tooth. I don't know whether it was purely psychological or what, but the pain seemed to subside, not totally, but bearable. I was so happy. I knew that I had to get hold of more of these tablets tomorrow or leave the village to go back to Pokhara to get some.

The next day, I set off to the health post with a new determination. I was not going to leave until I had some soluble aspirin in my possession. The health post only stocked basic health remedies, such as Vick, cough mixture and Strepsils, but I knew that there were soluble aspirin as I had seen them on the shelf next to the packets of Brufen. I flounced in, again, third time lucky I hoped. The assistant was not pleased to see me, but I was on a mission. I marched past her and took a box of soluble aspirin from the shelf. Written on the box in large writing was 'For throat ache. For leg ache. For body ache. For tooth ache.' It was there in black and white – for tooth ache. I thrust the box in front of her face. She was amazed. She had no idea that aspirin was used for this or throat ache. I gave her a quick lesson on how to dissolve aspirin to gargle with for relief from a sore throat, paid her for the box of tablets and left. Mission accomplished! The rest of my stay was relatively pain free. However, the incident did teach me to always carry soluble aspirin and antibiotics in my first aid kit.

Another incident where some aspects of it would have been bliss if ignorant, was when I had a particularly unpleasant fall. We had visited a place several hours away by road from Kathmandu. To leave this place a flight of metal steps had to be taken. It had been raining and I can remember saying to myself, "I must not slip on these steps". And with that, I slipped on the steps, very ungraciously. I twisted my knee, but I somehow landed with my foot in an awkward position, and it was extremely painful. I couldn't stay there in the rain, so I was helped up by my companions and was half carried to the car. As I sat during the journey in the back of the car, my foot started to swell badly, and the pain was getting worse. What made it worse was that the 'only 5 hours' journey took more than seven hours because of a lorry getting stuck on the single lane mountain road. Jean, my friend, had to endure my sweaty foot under her nose for all that time.

By the time I was back at the hotel in Kathmandu, the pain was getting unbearable, and my mind was working overtime as to what had happened to my foot. It must be broken. OMG, I will need to have an x-ray and a plaster-cast. Would they set it right? The next thing I knew I was on the floor with at least half a dozen people peering down at me. I had fainted. I am quite good at fainting. I can even do it without showing my underwear. Suddenly, a man was looking down at me and saying," it is OK, I am a doctor". The tourist doctor had been called out. Unceremoniously, I was taken to my room where the doctor inspected my foot. After manipulating and prodding it, he didn't seem too concerned about it until he said, "I don't think it is broken so there is no need to worry. It is not as if you are diabetic". "But I am", I replied. With that he went into a panic. "Oh dear, I should send you for an x-ray, but I won't send you because if I do, they will say that your foot is broken, even if it is not, and they might even cut your leg off". He certainly had a strange bedside manner. He opened his plastic carrier bag and took out a little pot. It was one of those photographic film containers. He took the top off and took out a grubby piece of cotton wool which was steeped in some sort of disinfectant and dabbed it on my foot. He then took out a thermometer and wiped it with the same cotton wool and shoved it in my mouth before I could say anything. That was bad enough, the thought of wiping germs off my feet onto the thermometer, but then I realised that the odd-looking thermometer was, in fact, a rectal one. He pulled out of his bag a small plastic bag of strips of tablets. I had to read what they were as he had not got his spectacles with him. It was getting worse! He proceeded to administer one after another to me. He gave me an enormous worm tablet. But I had only been in Nepal for three days, I insisted. "Better to be safe," he said. He then gave me a vitamin tablet, a calcium tablet, an antibiotic, an anti-inflammatory, and a painkiller. He insisted on watching me to be sure I swallowed them. He did not charge me for the consultation, but 'requested' a $20 tip. He would come back tomorrow, for free again, and with that he was gone.

True to his word, the doctor came back every day for four more days. Each time he repeated the process, dab of foot with cotton wool, temperature taken and tablets except for the worming one. Of course, each time was free, but with a $20 tip. During this time, the swelling of my foot was diminishing although I was still in pain when I put my foot down. On the last visit the doctor gave me the pot with cotton wool so that I could dab it on my injury for the next ten days. Then he was gone. I cannot say for sure that the doctor had 'cured' my foot or it was just time that did it. However, I did not get worms and I am quite sure that taking my temperature daily, with a thermometer that had been cleaned with the same cotton wool for all his patients, had built up lots of anti-bodies in my body.

Money matters

One of the more uncomfortable aspects of visiting countries like Nepal is having to deal with the deluge of people wanting to relieve you of your cash, either by selling something that you hadn't realised you desperately needed, or by men, women or children begging for money. I am totally aware that most people who do this are on the poverty line or even below the poverty line. It can be no fun whatsoever to walk the streets of Kathmandu for hours on end begging or trying to sell goods to tourists in order to feed your family that night, only to be turned down, totally ignored or even shouted at. It must be frustrating for people to accept that tourists are not willing to buy their goods or to give money, when they know that most have spent several hundreds of pounds on air tickets to get to Nepal. So, I admire their tenacity.

During my earlier visits to Nepal, I was extremely uneasy giving money to beggars. It was not so much that I didn't want to give money, it was more that I did not know how much to give. On my first visit to Kathmandu, I gave a beggar some coins, not knowing their value, and he looked at them with disgust. It put me off future contributions in case I did the same again. Saying that, all the travel guides advise that people do not give to beggars as it encourages them to beg. I use this as a mental excuse to try and save me from guilt when I walk past someone holding out their empty hand.

One of my first encounters with beggars was when I went to visit Pashupati Nath, the Hindu cremation temple.

I was keen to visit this place, as everyone I met said that I must go as it is truly amazing. It was about 4pm and raining, but I decided to take a taxi to have a quick look around. I arrived as it was just starting to go dark. As I got out of the taxi, the driver said that he would stay in that spot and would wait with the taxi until I was ready to leave. I was expecting to stay for about one hour. I wandered around aimlessly, but soon realised that it probably was not the best time or conditions to be there. I was the only Westerner, so felt conspicuous. It was raining heavily, and I was wearing my flipflops, so I was slipping everywhere, and it was really going dark. One of my initial sights was a body burning on a pyre. I have seen many since then, but 'my' first one was quite a shock. I could clearly make out the deceased person's feet and arms through the straw and flames. It is not a regular occurrence in England. Then, I felt very intrusive on such an auspicious occasion.

As I continued walking around, I was overwhelmed by so many fascinating and yet 'normal' day-to-day glimpses of the people who live and pray in this incredible complex of temples and shrines. After only about thirty minutes, I was feeling very uneasy and so turned around to go back to the taxi. As I got near to the taxi, there were at least ten beggars making their way towards me. They had spied their only tourist to visit this place in these conditions and time. Easy prey! I know this sounds like an exaggeration, but it wasn't at the time, I was reminded of the Michael Jackson video of Thriller, where the zombies are walking towards him and his girlfriend. I ran the last few steps to the taxi. The driver was fast asleep. I hammered on the window, but he wouldn't wake up. The beggars were getting nearer. I frantically hammered again and shouted to be let in. He must have heard my heart thudding because at last, he woke up and let me in. I threw myself on the back seat and told him to go - Now. As we drove away, I looked back at the beggars. They looked disappointed and I felt relieved but with a pang of guilt.

I am not sure whether I am getting blind to beggars but there does not seem to be as many now in Thamel as there were in my early days. However, there are still many beggars just on the edge of Thamel, where there are lots of businesspeople, and near to the expensive hotels. They tend to congregate near to one of the major traffic junctions. I have seen young children, aged about three or four or even younger, sitting alone in the gutter of a busy road, begging. I shudder to think of the physical and moral danger these children are in. Sometimes, there are mothers with very young children on the pavement begging. I can only imagine what their lives were like in order to drive the mothers to have to put themselves and their children in such vulnerable situations.

One of the more unpleasant forms of begging for me, are the street children of six years old to teenagers who knock on the car/taxi windows when stopped at a junction begging for money for food. Quite often, they appear to be crying and gesturing with their hands that they are hungry. When told that they are not getting any money, sometimes they will spit or tell you to "f*** off". I have later seen these same youngsters on the streets sniffing glue. I cannot judge them for this. For many, that is the only 'high' that their life deals them, but I do not want to contribute to this. I have also seen them give the money to an older youth, so they are not even keeping the money for themselves.

For many years, there has been a man affected by leprosy sitting at the junction. He has been very badly deformed with the disease, with loss of fingers and heavily bloodied bandaged half-feet. During my research for my PhD, I interviewed many beggars who were affected by leprosy. In general, many had no other way of getting money because their disabilities prevented them from any sort of work. It was interesting to hear that some people had reluctantly turned to begging, as a last resort, but claimed that after the initial shame and embarrassment, they found it quite lucrative as they earned more than an average farm labourer. Nepalese people are very generous, and particularly to beggars who they would usually give just a few rupees or paisa when walking by. It is also to appease the gods for personal better karma. However, it must have been very uncomfortable sitting on the stone ground in all weathers.

During my earlier visits, there was a lone beggar who patrolled the streets of Thamel. He, too, was extremely disfigured with the effects of leprosy. He walked with two crutches. He had no fingers, just a stump for a thumb and no feet to speak of. He had lost part of his nose, and he had obvious eye problems. He carried a cloth bag around his neck for money he collected from the tourists. Perhaps it was my imagination, but I felt that we had some sort of connection. He would always call out to me, "Hiya sailor", and I would repeat the same back. I started to give him my left-over change each evening. I could see that his physical condition was deteriorating over the years. One day, I asked how he was. He rolled his trouser legs up and showed me his legs and rubbed them. He intimated that they were sore. They looked very red. I commiserated with him. I had seen what leprosy infection could do to the limbs.

The next year he was not to be seen on the streets. I felt really sad as I thought that he might have died. Then, blow me, the following year I heard someone call 'Hiya sailor', he was back. I went over to him and told him how pleased I was to see him. I asked after his legs. He again rolled up his trousers and there were a pair of prosthetic legs. He knocked on them and looked so thrilled. I was delighted for him. I gave him some change and he set off down the street with a proud, if not cocky, stride in his gait. I watched him go with a tear in my eye. He suddenly stopped, turned around and saluted, then he was gone. I will never forget that man.

Regular beggars to Thamel are women with babies in arms, possibly up to 18 months old. They arrive in Thamel early in the morning by the truck load. It is doubtful that the babies are their own babies but are used to pull at heart strings for cash. Quite often they will have a handwritten letter in English on one side and Nepali on the other, saying how they have been left on their own by their husband and they have no money to look after the baby. I have no doubt whatsoever that these women are poor, but it is believed that any money given to them is passed onto a ringleader, not to feed the baby. I usually go to the nearest bakery and buy two rolls or fruit and give them directly to the woman and baby and watch them eat until all gone.

Another trick, using the notion of babies, is when children or sometimes women approach with empty feeding bottles and ask if you could buy some milk for the starving baby at home. I fell for this one as they are so plausible. You are taken to a shop that sells milk. Whilst expecting to buy a bottle of milk for the baby, you finish up buying a giant bag of powdered milk. It is doubtful that the milk went to the family but was sold for cash. I do not like to be duped but I would like to think that the cash, or at least some of the milk, goes to the family.

Not all people who prise money out of tourists are street traders or beggars. Many are just opportunistic, who see a chance to benefit from gullible tourists, like me. And why not? I had read and been told many times that a photo opportunity might have to be paid for. Nepal is a photographer's dream. You can drop your camera on the floor and still get a beautiful photo as it falls. Everywhere is so interesting and photogenic. When I first went to Nepal, I was clicking at nearly everything I saw. I couldn't help myself.

One day I was visiting Durbar Square where some of the most incredibly iconic and majestic temples were situated. After a while I sat on a low wall, just to take in the ambiance of the place. You don't have to be religious to be able to feel the spirituality of Nepal. It was so peaceful in the square. It did not last long, I was soon joined by four children, about nine years old. A couple of them spoke good English and we chatted for a while. I enjoyed the conversations.

Suddenly, out of the blue, stood a man in long orange robes, lots of face paint, long dreadlocked hair, and carrying a trident. As it was my first visit to Nepal, I had bought a copy of the Lonely Planet Guide. In it was a photograph of this very same man. He was a holy man or Sadhu. I was overjoyed. He asked me if I would like a photo of him. Would I, OMG what a catch! How kind of him. He posed for me, looking just like the photo in the book. I couldn't believe my luck. Suddenly, his face changed from the smiley sadhu to a hard, somewhat frightening mask. "Rupees, give me rupees", he growled. I looked at the children who looked uneasy and asked what I should do. They said, "He wants you to pay for his photograph. You must do or he will get nasty". At that point, I was in a quandary, how much do I give? I opened my purse and said to him, "How much?" Can you believe that someone can be so naïve? "$20", he said. He must have thought that all his Diwalis had come in one go. The '$20' pulled me together. I certainly was not that daft. I pulled out a 100Rs note, which was about 70p, and told him to go. It was my turn to be assertive. I stood up and repeated that he should go - now. With that he was off. I learned later that he was not a genuine holy man but in fact a university lecturer who supplemented his income by approaching tourists as a sadhu.

He was not the only person to pretend to be, or use his status, as a religious man to deprive tourists of money. I have spoken before about Pashupati Nath, the Hindu cremation temple. It is a curious complex of buildings, but also brimming with fascinating people. In many of the small temples are genuine sadhus who have given up their homes, lives, and possessions in order to achieving mokṣa, or liberation. Most of the sadhus are genuine and dress in orange robes, as the 'holy man' in Durbar Square. Many are also covered in grey ashes. Some of them do beg or charge for photos, but just enough for bare necessities, such as food. They make a splendid display of colour at the temple.

On several occasions, I have been approached by a regular looking man who offered me something that I have never been offered before. He wanted to know if I would be interested in visiting a sadhu who could show me how he can lift a rock up with his penis, for a small price of course. Each time I have declined, although I went with a friend once who told the man that her husband did that every morning. She was joking of course, I think. I have since spoken to tourists who have taken up the offer from the sadhu. They claim that he has not lifted 'a rock' but has managed to lift a large bag. Perhaps I am being a bit unkind, but I think it is quite sad for a human being to spend his time building up the strength, and I suppose the length, of his penis.

As I have said before, Nepal is so interesting that I wanted to take photos of everything to show back home. Again, on my first trip, I was roaming around the streets of Kathmandu and got lost. That never bothered me as I just had to ask someone where Kathmandu Guest House was which was used as a marker point. Everyone knew Kathmandu Guest House as it was the first hotel in Kathmandu many years ago.

Anyway, I came across a 'water tank'. It was sunken into the ground and this one was about 10 feet squared. Stone steps were built on all sides. Three spouts protruded from one of the walls, with a continuous pouring of fresh, clean water. There were several women using the tank. Some were filling metal jugs to take back home, some were washing their clothes, some their bodies, including the children, and some were rinsing their pots and pans. For me it was a most wonderful scene. At the university, I taught about water provision. This was a must for a photograph. I stood quite a way back in order to get the whole scene in and clicked.

Suddenly, a woman waved frantically from the tank. I had not noticed her as I was not focusing on anyone in particular. She was sitting on one of steps and was holding a baby with another young child sitting next to her. "Hello lady", she shouted out. "Rupees". I was in a predicament because I genuinely did not have any money on me. She stood up and with her baby in her arms and a child literally hanging onto her skirt, she started to run to me. I panicked and started to run away. She followed me, shouting "Rupees, rupees for photo". I kept running but it was very wet under foot, and I was wearing those wretched flipflops again. My feet kept slipping out of them. I took them off and kept running until I lost her. What a coward I was!

After that I became quite proficient at taking photos of people by making it look as if I was really engrossed in a telegraph pole or some form of drainage work. However, I have given my share of money to people for photos, if I wanted an image of a specific person doing a specific activity. It is only right. And there are certain occasions when I would never dream of taking photos, such as when people are praying or bathing privately. I would never take photos of someone's room without permission, and never photograph the inside of a temple. Whilst I would possibly photograph someone laughing, I would not dream of doing so if someone is crying. I do try to be sensitive and ethical.

Nepal is a buyer's paradise. Whatever you want, you can either buy on the streets or someone will know where to get it, cheap. ANYTHING! Every year when I walk from my hotel into Thamel, I am asked by several men if I want 'to smoke' or if I want some hashish. Of course, I turn it down. I have never smoked cigarettes, let alone smoked weed. Not because I am a prude, but because I am a coward.

I must admit that I did like to be offered it as it made me feel that I looked cool and had the saunter of a hippy. I always admired people who dressed and acted how they wanted, without following the trends of the time or their age. I was in my mid-teens in the 1960s when 'flower power' was all the rage and hippies dominated the media. I desperately wanted to be a hippy. I would wear my hair long and down, with flowers fastened to it, very mini dresses with flowers sewn onto them, and sometimes bare feet. I would stroll down the main street in my small market town, thinking I was spreading love and peace. Unfortunately, the townsfolk did not think the same and I had to endure sniggers and outright ridicule. Looking back, I can understand why; I did look very much out of place, and I was actually following a trend, not so much a conventional one, but a trend all the same. However, I have never got over my pseudo-hippy phase, and so, when in Nepal, I usually revert back to my youth with long flowing clothes, (I couldn't get away with mini dresses now) and try to portray an aura of peace and tranquillity. I am probably deluded, but it does make me feel younger.

A couple of years ago I was not approached to buy hashish, and I felt disappointed. I must be looking like a conventional elderly woman, or even worse, a normal tourist. I became quite depressed and had a mini- identity crisis. However, the following year my swagger must have come back because I was stopped several times to purchase 'hashish'. I was so pleased to say "no".

One woman I remember from my early visits to Thamel used to sit at the side of the road in the very centre of Thamel selling cigarettes, in packets or singly. She would sit there day and night, regardless of weather. If it was raining, she would put a plastic bag over her stall, which was basically a small sheet on the floor, and hold an umbrella over her head. She was cheerful and seemed to be popular and busy. The next year that I saw her she had had a baby. He was still being cradled, so she just popped him under her top so he could feed and to stay warm. She was positioned at a terribly busy junction where lots of traffic would stop, including cars, taxis, motor bikes and auto-rickshaws. Consequently, they were both exposed to continuous fuel pollution. The following year, she was still there and so was her baby, who now was at the toddling stage. I was surprised to see that she had tied a rope around the boy's neck and the other end around her own ankle, in order for him not to run off. For the next couple of years, the rope stayed on the child as he developed into a mischievous youngster. Yes, I was shocked at first. It is easy to judge people against your own standards. But what else could the mother do? She had to work. She had no one to look after her child. She wanted to keep him safe and near, so the rope was her only course of action, and it did the trick. I am not sure that I would have done anything differently if I was in her position.

Another young man (I will call him Chet) used to stand in the hub of Thamel with a tray selling thalis, little cloth purses fastened with a draw string. His wife sat next to him making the thalis. I went over to him and waited to buy one while he served another tourist. The tourist picked up a few pieces and asked how much. Chet obviously had no numeracy skills because he gave the tourist a ridiculously low figure, something like 20Rs instead of 200Rs. Fortunately, the tourist was honest and paid him the right price. I was really concerned how vulnerable Chet was.

After that time, I would visit him often when in the vicinity. He had a speech defect, and his English was poor, but we managed to communicate somehow. He worked really hard to sell his goods and his wife was always with him. He started to sell pencil cases. He also started to use a calculator, which I was relieved about. I had not started my business then, so I would buy just the odd thing for gifts. They were good quality, so I was pleased with my purchases. One year I went to seek Chet out and he was not there. I was told that the police had come and stopped him trading as he did not have the proper paperwork for his small tray of goods. They had confiscated all his wares leaving him with nothing. I don't know how they sleep at night.

I have been to Nepal so many times that many of the street sellers in Thamel know me and so do not try to sell me their wares. I have built up quite a good relationship with the men who sell the saringhis, wooden violin-type instruments. They are of the Gandharba caste, a musician caste. Many are from the east of Nepal, which is one of the more impoverished areas of Nepal. They are quite a cheerful group and spend their time walking the streets of Thamel whilst playing their saringhis. They also sell CDs with music recorded at their concerts that they play at the various restaurants around Kathmandu. I bought a saringhi on my first visit and purchased several CDs over the years. This group now know that I will not be coaxed into buying anymore. As a result, whenever they see me now, we stop and have a chat like old friends.

However, their patter to buy their goods has changed to telling me stories of their life. Most of it is money related, such as one mother-in-law needed money for anti-biotics, another had been promised money by a tourist for his son to attend school and it never materialised. Post-earthquake was particularly heart-wrenching, with numerous tales of losing everything they possessed. I am not naïve to believe every story, but I could soon wheedle out the real and exaggerated stories. I decided from early on in my travels that I would not give money to individuals on the street. It is so tempting when you know that you could take out of your back pocket the money to solve some of their problems. But it would be like opening a can of worms.

However, for the past few years I have been giving one of the men, I will call him Lal, something to take to his village. He had been telling me about his community and how poor everyone was. Diwali was coming up and he had nothing to take back to his village as gifts. Before going out to Nepal I usually gather bits and pieces such as children's clothes, blankets, medication to give to various causes I support. My local bank has been exceedingly kind by giving me a box or two of pens, each box contained 200 pens. I met Lal in Thamel. I took a box of the pens out of my bag and gave them to him. He looked amazed. I told him that he must take the pens to his village for the school. He said, "Can I give one each to my children?" Of course, I said. "Can I give one each to my neighbours' children?" Of course. "And then can I give one each to my brothers' children?" Of course, I said again. "And can I...." I knew where this was going. "Stop, you can give one to anyone you like, I trust you". He was so happy, and I felt humbled that something like a box of Barclays pens would be so important. The next year I went back to Thamel and met Lal again. He ran over to me as soon as he saw me. "I took the pens to the village". "Good", I said. "Yes, I gave one each to each of my children. They were so happy. Then one each to my neighbours' children, and then my brother's children, then ....". "Yes, I get the idea. Thank you for doing that for me. Here are some more" and pulled another box out of my bag for him and left before he told me who he was going to give them to.

Most people selling services or goods on the streets can be extremely persistent. I have been followed back to my hotel before now by a trader when I looked remotely interested in buying an elephant- not a real one, of course. Another day a young man stalked me, offering to polish my plastic flip flops.

Indeed, there is no need to walk anywhere in Kathmandu as there is always a rickshaw within a few feet of you, offering 'a very good price' to have a tour of the city or to get you to your hotel. I have been followed for long distances by rickshaw drivers trying to get me to take a ride. In fact, I have got out of a taxi at my hotel and immediately been approached to take a rickshaw to the hotel door. I do feel sorry for these men. It must be so strenuous for them to cycle around Kathmandu with heavy bags or several people loaded onto the small rickshaw seats, with tatty umbrellas to protect them from the elements. To many, these are also their homes to be slept in throughout the night. Indeed, the cycles are often poorly maintained and run to the ground. I once had the interesting experience of sitting on one when one of the wheels dropped off. I am still not sure how I did not fall out of it! At least there was another rickshaw nearby to help me to finish my journey.

There is a young woman who I meet up with every year in Thamel. She is petite with a pretty face that is always smiling. Many years ago, I bought a small cloth bag from her for about £1. She was very persuasive with her spiel and charm. I did actually need one of the bags. Every year since then she has 'found' me in Thamel and tried to sell me more bags and purses. Now she greets me as if we were sisters, by flinging her arms around my waist and hugging me tightly. As it happens, I am a regular customer now that I have my small business. I usually sell on market stalls or craft fairs. I suppose you could say that I, too, was a street trader and so we should show solidarity. Consequently, I usually purchase something like ten bags and ten purses. She is so happy but not enough to stop her suggesting I take more and more. You cannot blame her for trying.

Bargaining is part of the game played out between the buyer and seller. It is expected to happen, except in certain shops where you will be put right the first time you try it. I was at the local market and asked the price of a bracelet. I was told £20. "Too much". "£18". "No too much. It is ok, I will leave it". And walked off. "No, madam. I will give it for £15". "No thank you, I will have to think about it". I walked quickly but she followed me, and at regular intervals she dropped the price, eventually reaching £5. By then, I really didn't want it, but I felt embarrassed for the woman as she was begging me. She must have been desperate, so I gave in and bought it. I know that was her plan at the onset, but needs must. Anyway, the bracelet broke within a couple of days, so she won the game. I must try harder.

In my experience, Tibetan women were the most persistent street sellers, especially in my early visits. They were evident in Pokhara, where there are at least two Tibetan refugee camps. The women, usually in pairs, would be wearing traditional Tibetan dress with the characteristic stripped apron. They did not appear to have anything to sell. They always had a welcoming smile and usually approached their 'victims' as if they wanted to make friends, especially if you were having a rest or dining outside a restaurant. Most Tibetans I have met speak impeccable English, which made it quite simple to draw a conversation. I was an easy target as I was normally on my own. When they had gained trust, the women would then suddenly open their apron and, lo and behold, reveal a whole cache of sparkling bracelets, necklaces, rings and more. "Would you like to buy something for yourself or your daughter? Very good prices only for you because we are now friends". Often, I would be given a cotton friendship bracelet as a token of our newfound relationship. They are so canny! I am easily beaten down and buy something at a greatly 'just for me' reduced price to enable me to escape. Saying that, my weakness is jewellery. I never buy expensive jewellery, but I do like unusual styles or colours. The Tibetans do make some nice pieces.

I think it was on my second visit to Pokhara that there seemed to be swarm of Tibetan sellers. I was approached by two women who gave me the usual pitch and started to show me their collection. I stopped them. "I am not going to look now, as tomorrow I will be going to Ghandruk and so do not buy anything before trekking". "But you will buy when you come back?" "Possibly. I will look". That shut them up. The next day I went to Ghandruk and was there for two weeks.

I have told you about how my journeys up and down the foothills are torturous for me. I was nearly at the end of my journey back to Naya Pul when I staggered into the village of Biritanthi. In those days, it was a small place with a few restaurants and shops, about one or two miles from Naya Pul. I arrived there absolutely exhausted, my legs shaking, not sure what part of my body hurt the most, sweat pouring through my clothes, and my throat felt as dry as the Sahara Desert. I threw myself at a table and chair in one of the restaurants. If I could just rest and close my eyes for a few minutes I would feel that I could finish the journey.

Suddenly, and this is no word of a lie, I heard a familiar voice. "My friend, we waited for you. Would you like to buy now?" I thought I must be having some hallucination due to dehydration and fatigue. But no, standing in front of me were the two Tibetan women that I had been talking to before going to Ghandruk, smiling like Cheshire cats and apron open displaying their trinkets. I honestly thought that I was going mad. This couldn't be true. Through gasps of breath, I said in a quiet scream, if that is possible, "No. I don't want to buy from you. Can't you see I am nearly dead?" "That is Ok my friend, we will wait until you feel better". "No, no, no. I don't want to buy and (the old nugget) I don't have any money on me." "It is OK, my friend, we know your hotel so you can pay us when you get back to Pokhara". Fortunately, at this stage the waitress came along and told the women to leave me alone. I was so grateful. I had my sustenance, and when the coast was clear as the women were 'charming' some other trekkers, I left quickly. I breathed a sigh of relief as I assumed that I would not have to encounter the women again.

The next morning, I decided to go on the Phewa Tal, the lake. I came out of my hotel, and I couldn't believe my eyes; there were the Tibetan women sitting under a tree, just outside the hotel. I knew I had to act quickly. So, I raced passed them and shouted I had an appointment so couldn't stop. They shouted that they would wait. I told them not to as I did not know how long I would be. Some wise person said, 'Necessity is the mother of invention'. I spent my last two days in Pokhara, inventing different routes to my hotel in order to avoid them. I hope that they did eventually move on and find another prey. They were not bad women, just making a living.

On my latest visit to Nepal, my husband came with me, as I have said before. On our first full day in Kathmandu, we walked past a small barber's shop. Rod had not had time, before flying out, to have his hair cut. Jokingly, I said let's get your hair cut here and he agreed. I was amazed. We told the barber that he only wanted a quick haircut. "OK" he said and sat Rod down in a chair and put a grubby towel around him. Rod was follically challenged, so the

124

trim did not take long, but the barber did a good job. The barber then covered Rod's chin with shaving foam and gave him a cutthroat razor shave, followed by threading his eyebrows and shaving the hair growing out of Rod's nose and ears. (He will hate me for telling you that!) I was waiting for Rod to retaliate as he did not like 'that sort of thing', but he took it. Next, he scraped his skin with a piece of cotton thread, followed by creaming his face and scraping it again. The barber insisted on showing me the dirt coming out of his pores. It is a good job that we had been married for 50 years! He then covered Rod's face with pink powder and left it on while he gave him a vigorous face, head and shoulder massage. The barber finished off by cleaning the powder off with the dirty towel. I must admit that Rod looked really good afterwards. His skin was so much brighter. I was impressed even though we had only asked for a haircut.

I decided that I would have my eyebrows threaded as they had not been done for a long time. I insisted that I only wanted my eyebrows threaded, nothing else. The barber agreed so he started. He was very quick and proficient, and I was pleased with the results, but he was on a roll. He gave me the full facial treatment that he had done on Rod. He started to do the massage on my head, neck, and shoulders. He was so brutal with it. He must have had a row with his wife that morning. I had to stop him as I have arthritis in some of my neck vertebrae and my shoulders, so the pain was unbearable. He wiped off the pink powder with the dirty towel he had used on Rod. When asked how much for the service, he said about £60! What! You must be joking. We only asked for one haircut and one threading. He dropped the price down to £40. My husband, who does not like a fuss and was not used to bargaining, paid up. I felt that the barber had ripped us off but, at the same time he had given us a really good make over. After 26 years I should have known better to ask the price first. You can't win them all!!!

When I had been going to Nepal for three or four years, I came up with a cunning plan to stop street traders from harassing me. Most of the time I can cope with people trying to help me to spend my money. I usually politely say, "No, thank you" and then turn my head away. This tended to be my usual tactic. The key is not to hesitate at all and not to look them in the eyes. If you do, then you have lost. You will be followed or begged. However, I started to play them at their own game. If harassed too much, I would fetch my comb or suchlike out of my bag and hold it up. "You want to buy my comb? Very cheap price. Real plastic. You buy?" That usually stopped them in their tracks. They did not know if I was joking or for real. "But didi, it is a comb". "Yes, that is right. You want to buy it?" With that the sellers went away in total confusion. I used this method several times during that stay, on many sellers. I must admit I did get some very strange looks, but it worked.

Then one day I had a walk down to Durbar Square. It was out of season and so I was one of very few tourists in Nepal. I was wandering around the square, when I was surrounded by at least six street sellers trying to sell me tiger balm, beads, tablas (small hand drums), candy floss on a stick, shawls, and even sunglasses. I stopped dead, put my hand in my bag and pulled out my comb. One of the sellers must have recognised me from Thamel, and shouted, "It is her. She is a mad woman". With that, they all ran away from me. I did not know whether to be offended by being called a mad woman or be pleased by my success. Let's say I had a pleasurable stroll around the square with no harassment, so I suppose if I was offended it didn't last too long. I did try this ploy the following year, but I must have lost my touch, because people just laughed. *C'est la vie!*

It is the way that you say it

Communication is particularly important during my visits to Nepal, as it is for anyone visiting foreign countries. A great deal of frustration and upset can happen if what you are trying to convey to others is misinterpreted, whether it is what you say, or how you say it. Because of my lack of spoken Nepali, I often resort to actions, word play, or even acting out. I have been known to stage a whole show, with props, in order to go over something that had happened to me, much to the amusement of my audience. Communication would be so much easier if I had learnt to speak Nepali. My excuse, when I am asked why I do not speak Nepali after all these years, is to say that it would be unfair to learn just one of the languages in Nepal as there are so many. I do not want to offend any particular ethnic group. That is my excuse, and I am sticking to it.

In truth, languages were never my strong point. I twice failed French O' level at school after learning it for 6 years and, even worse, I failed German despite having a German mother. So, it is of no surprise but of great embarrassment that after 26 years of annual visits to Nepal, my Nepali language continues to be extremely minimal. I longed to talk to people in their own language on a casual and one to one basis. I had met such an array of amazing people with whom I would loved to have a chat.

My lack of language skills has meant that I have had to rely on interpreters for most of my interviews with the women in Ghandruk during my independent study research and with the majority of people affected by leprosy for my

PhD. I am truly grateful for their services but sometimes it could lead to frustration. There were times when I would ask a simple question, such as, "Do you think it is more important for you to have a son more than a daughter?". The interpreter and interviewee would have a very long and intense conversation. I became quite excited about the rich data I would get from this interview. After about ten minutes, I but in to ask what the answer was, expecting a detailed response. "No" was the answer. "But you have been talking for a long time, so I thought there would be a long answer. What did she say?" "Oh, we were just talking about a mutual friend and her family". This sort of exchange happened often. Many times, I have felt extremely rude when I have butted into a conversation that my friends were having in Nepali, as I was not sure that the conversation or even a sentence has stopped.

However, it is incredible how conversations can be had without a common language. I have had many chats with women about family life, problems with children and other domestic issues. It can be done somehow, using gestures as I have said earlier, including facial expressions. I always have photos on me of my family. I have learnt their names (not Rod, Paul, Claire), that is, their relationships in Nepali, such as 'husband', 'son', 'daughter'. These kinds of 'chats' were very important to me to break down barriers of 'them 'and 'us', which made it easier to have open and honest conversations if we saw each other as living, breathing, normal people with similarities.

Even when I have had conversations with English - speaking Nepalis, I have learnt that I have to speak slower and clearer than my usual babble. And in many cases I have to remember not to use idioms and, which is difficult for me, not to include sarcasm. I had to stop asking footless or wheelchair-bound leprosy patients if they believe that they will stand on their own two feet. Of course, I meant economically! It was not the most sensitive question I had asked. I did have to intervene when an English friend asked some school children what they were doing when they 'broke up' [from school]. Some seemed somewhat concerned with the question, I am sure they must have thought that their arms and legs would drop off and have been left traumatised for life! I don't think that we are aware of how much we use idioms.

In an attempt to be self-sufficient, several years ago, I enrolled on a basic Nepali language course in Kathmandu. At the language centre I was greeted by a cheerful Chinese man who was giving English lessons to Nepali people. In my opinion, it was not a great match as even I had difficulty understanding him. The woman who was going to give me personal tuition in Nepali turned out to be quite an ogre, not at all like the sweet gentle woman she claimed to be when I first met her to book the course. She reminded me of my old English teacher at school, Miss Lakin. She petrified me just with her stare. I went for lessons for 6 days, starting at 6 am- with a test at the end. Serious stuff! There was no laughing and very stern reactions when I got a phrase, sentence, or word wrong. In fact, I dreaded the lessons and was relieved when they came to an end. I passed the test – I did not dare to fail. However, as shown in the next few short experiences, the lessons had not been a great success for me.

I had been on a visit outside the Kathmandu Valley and was on the way back when my transport broke down – if I recall the wheel fell off. After a long wait for another wheel, I felt hungry and so trotted off to a little shop near-by. I picked up a small packet of biscuits and in my best Nepali, held them up and asked the shop keeper "Kosta chhaa". He looked puzzled. Ok, if I say it louder he will understand me as I ask him "How much?" "Kosta chhaa". Still no recognition of what I was asking. His wife arrived and had the same look on her face but with an added strained smile. Then the children came. These were not inhibited. They actually laughed. Surely asking the price of a packet of biscuits was not that amusing. Everyone was now laughing at me – me who had a whole 6 days of Nepali language lessons. I must be correct. My driver arrived and put me right. Oh dear, it turned out that I was asking the shop keeper "if he was OK?", not the price. We all burst out laughing. I was excused, I was English!

Pronunciation was another factor in my failure to verbally communicate clearly with Nepalese people. I blame my North Staffordshire accent rather than my prowess at the language – after all, I have had 6 days of Nepali language lessons. Not sure I have mentioned it before.

One of my favourite places in Kathmandu is Indra Chowk in the traditional part of the city. It is at the junction of five roads and is bustling with cars, taxis, rickshaws, the odd cow, and people and street vendors selling scarves, jewellery, flutes, tabla, Tiger Balm, saringhi and much more. It is obviously a marketplace for the 'locals' and an attraction to tourists on their way to the main Durbar

Square. Two of the roads sell mainly 'modern' goods such as TVs, phones, computers, western style clothes, whereas the other roads are lined with shops selling more 'traditional' goods such as material, Nepali clothes, gold jewellery, kitchen ware and household equipment. Tailoring shops are found down some of the narrow alleyways. The whole area is noisy and chaotic but so vibrant and exciting.

One day I visited one of the tailors to be measured for a kurta surawal (tunic and pants), a traditional ladies' outfit. It was somewhat embarrassing being measured by a man in the open shop front who shouted out my 'inches' to his assistant with several passers-by stopping to watch. Fortunately, I was getting used to being stared at, and unfortunately, being described as 'moti' – fat. After the indignity of public scrutiny, I went around the corner and chose some material for the tunic and some coordinating material for the pants. I picked a beautiful black material with large red flowers and yellow leaves for the tunic and deep red for the pants. Additionally, it is custom to wear a matching scarf, so I chose a red one. It was coming up for Teej, the women's festival, where married women wore red and gold costumes. This was my chance to blend in!

All I needed now were matching beads for my neck and wrists. At Indra Chowk I was shown the bead market tucked behind some shops. It would have been easy to miss as the cramped entrance was nestled between an umbrella shop and underwear stall. Wow! The market consisted of dozens of small cubicles with cross-legged Muslim men surrounded by skeins of shiny beads of multiple colours and sizes, and designs of jewellery. I know this sounds like a cliché, but it was like walking into Aladdin's cave.

I had wanted red beads to exactly match my new outfit. I was keen to get the matching tone of red. A friend had told me the word in Nepali for beads, 'potey', so I was confident enough to shop for them on my own. I went to one of the cubicles and asked for the specific colour of beads 'red puti'. I was slightly taken back by the lack of enthusiasm from the sellers. In fact, as I went from one stall to another many men turned away or even smirked. Was it because I was a woman? No, most customers were women. Was it because I was a Westerner? No, as I had not experienced any discrimination in Nepal before. Perhaps I was not shouting loud enough – it was busy and noisy there. I tried again but louder and emphasising the words 'red puti'. Still the same reaction. Huh!!! Eventually I picked up some beads as near to as I wanted and turned-tail out of there, vowing never to go back again.

The next day I met my Nepali friend and related my woeful story of the 'red puti' to her. I looked on incredulously as she started to choke and then laugh and then became hysterical with laughter. Tears rolled down her face and she was clutching her stomach with pain. Eventually she calmed down enough to blurt out that my pronunciation was not quite right. In fact, I had been asking for red female genitals (puti) not beads (potey). Oh dear, I suppose an easy mistake to make.

I have to say that some Nepalese people use the lack of language skills in visitors to their own advantage. It has been known that they pretend not to know what we are saying in order to profit from us. A classic example for me was when I rented a doonga (boat) and a rower for a boat ride on Phewa Tal, the lake at Pokhara. The fee was by the hour. It was extremely hot that day and I did not want to go on the doonga for more than one hour. I paid at the kiosk and got onto the boat. The lake has an amazing backdrop of Annapurna and Fishtail mountains, which were reflected in the water. Along the far side of the lake was an expanse of stunning thick trees and bushes. In the middle of the lake was a small temple that was popular with Nepalis and visitors to the town. It was impossible not to feel at peace amid the picturesque landscape.

I had been on a doonga before, so I knew roughly how long it takes to row from one point to another. We set off. I put my umbrella over my head to shade from the powerful sun and let my mind drift off. All I could hear were the rhythmically splashing of the oars in the water, the birds, and the piercing sound of the insects in the trees. Very hypnotizing.

As we were 45 minutes into my one-hour boat ride, I became conscious that we were quite away from the landing point. There was no way that we would get back in 15 minutes. I tried to tell my rower, who incidentally was a woman, that we needed to get back. I pointed to my watch and the other side of the lake. I was sure that she had not realised the time. But no reaction. It was as if I wasn't there. I tried again to tell her. She just carried on rowing, further away from the landing point. I was getting more and more frustrated, but she did not bat an eyelid. By then, I was ridiculously hot, sweaty, and desperate for the loo. I became assertive. In my best 'teacher voice' and using mime, I demanded that we return to the landing point, now, this minute. She looked at her watch, shrugged and steered the doonga towards the right way. After two hours from setting off, we arrived at the landing point, and I got off. I was not a happy woman, which intensified when I was asked for another one-hour payment because I was over my prescribed time. The rower knew exactly what she was doing. I was annoyed but at the same time, secretly admired her use of fake ignorance.

In case you were wondering whether my bladder held out or not after my little excursion, I rushed to the public toilet. Next to a man sitting outside with toilet paper, there was a big sign for all to see, so there was no breakdown of communication, saying: 'PISS, 1Rs, SHIT, 2Rs'. Unfortunately, there was no set charge for 'not sure'.

Whilst it can be a good game to have fun with language, it does not always end well. My experience of Nepalese people, especially in Kathmandu, is that they are keen to learn English, even if it is the odd word. Many of the traders in Thamel, the tourist area in Kathmandu, can speak good English or at least a smattering of it, to help them in their businesses. I am full of admiration for their fortitude and embarrassed for my laziness.

One day I was on a quest to buy some incense sticks for gifts for my friends. They were sold in many of the shops in Thamel, but I like to buy from street traders because they need to sell their wares daily to pay for food that night. They do not get wages. On one of the streets was a man with a small table on which he had an array of incense sticks. Just the job! I proceeded to pick up sticks and sniff them, one at a time. As I did it, the man said, "Disgusting". I thought that it was quite pleasant, but I put it down and picked another one to sniff. "Disgusting", he said again, and with every stick I smelled he said the same. I thought that it was refreshing to meet a trader who was so honest about his goods but at the same time I was concerned that he would not get many sales. Eventually I asked him why he said that they were all disgusting. With a big smile, he claimed that a tourist had told him that they were and advised him to tell his customers. I explained to him that a better word was 'nice' or 'beautiful'. He seemed happy with that. I bought several packets of his 'nice' incense sticks and left. This is an example of when a 'joke' can go too far and have the potential to ruin someone's business.

Earlier on in this section, I had told you of my disconcerting mistake of mispronouncing a Nepali word, leading to a very embarrassing situation. However, I have had an incident once where a Nepali receptionist also became muddled with two English words. I had been put on some strong antibiotics for dysentery which I was to take every four hours, even through the night. As I went to bed that night, I asked the receptionist, who had a reasonably good command of English, to wake me at 2 am because I had to take medication. He agreed and wrote it down on his note pad. The next morning, I was surprised to see that I had slept right through, and it was eight o'clock. I had not had my wake-up call at 2 am. I went down to the receptionist who was still on duty. "What happened to my wake-up call? Did you forget?". "No, didi. But I thought it was pointless to wake you up from sleeping for you to do meditation". An easy mistake to make!

Life changing

By now, I think that you have gathered that some of my experiences have been challenging for me, to say the least. Most have been a trial because of my inexperience, naivety, lack of physical fitness, and downright stubbornness to keep going. However, much of it has been because I was too embarrassed to say "No". Thank goodness that that was the case because I needed pushing into doing anything new. I lacked confidence in my own abilities most of the time, which has held me back from being more adventurous in the past.

My experiences in Nepal have shown me that I am capable of stepping out of my comfort zone. I have done things that I would never have dreamt of doing back home. I would never have entertained the thought of going on extremely poorly built roads on mountain tracks in substandard vehicles in the UK, nor on a mule. I certainly would never have walked through a jungle on my own or climbed into a lorry with four strange men. I would never have allowed a strange man to approach me in the street in my city and walk with me, just to practise his English. I had to learn to trust people when they were nice to me, with no hidden agenda. It is sad, but also a sign of the times that we must be so cynical.

When I first went to work in Ghandruk all those years ago, one of the managers of the organisation said to me, "You will be getting more out of being here than we will get out of you". At the time, I was rather taken back and offended by his arrogance. I was giving my time for free and had paid a lot of money for the pleasure of it. However, I soon realised that he was totally right. OK, I worked in the nursery and would like to think that I had contributed in a positive way. I have raised bits of money for various causes and have spent money on my business, thus helping Nepali economy. But none of that can compare to the experiences that I have had, good and bad. My research in Ghandruk enabled me to attain a decent grade in my independent studies. Digging into peoples' lives allowed me to present a good thesis and to become a 'doctor'. Indeed, just visiting this beautiful country had enhanced my understanding of all manner of Third World issues.

Over so many years, I have gained much knowledge of Nepal and its people. Every year I am astounded to learn something new about their customs or way of life. I have also seen many changes, particularly working practices and infrastructure in the urban areas. Modern buildings pop up from nowhere and roads are widened to accommodate lorries. Workers appear to have more rights, and health and safety regulations are imposed, although rarely implemented. The health of the nation is undoubtably much improved since my first visits, with less children dying at an early age due to uptake of vaccination programmes and better awareness of health issues. Unfortunately, there is still a long way to go, particularly in more traditional and remote parts of Nepal where access to health care and education is still lacking.

I sometimes have trouble getting my head around the fact that many families have modern smart phones yet have no latrines or safe water provision. I then need to question myself, who am I to say what provision is the most important to someone living in the hills who wants to have regular contact with their children who live in Kathmandu. I have had to stop comparing 'them' to 'us', with Western values and eyes. There is still so much to learn about this amazing country, although, I do think that I will never master the language or get my head around the intricacies of Hinduism and Buddhism.

Nepal is an incredibly beautiful country, with iconic buildings and, of course, the stunning mountains and scenery. But for me the Nepalese people really are the attraction of this country. People who I had never met before invited me into their homes and into their lives. Their generosity and warmth have no bounds. I know that it is a cliché to say that 'The people are so poor, yet they would give you their last mouthful of food'. But, in many cases, they would. At the same time those who are comfortably off seem to open their homes and welcome constant visitors who they feed or allow to stay for a night or more. Indeed, it is often difficult to tell who permanently live in some homes and who are just passing through. Even my regular hotel staff in Kathmandu welcome me so warmly and are so kind. I truly feel that I am going to my other 'home' when I fly into Kathmandu. I think that my feeling of ease when I am in Nepal is because I know that I will be looked after by one of my 'families'.

I have been privileged to be given opportunities that no regular tourist would have been afforded, such as visiting leprosy institutions and hospitals. One of my magical visits was to a leprosy village. It was like visiting a regular village and family but with many people being very deformed.

There was so much banter and laughter that the disfigurements became invisible.

On another occasion I was able to watch a dance therapy class in a hospital for people with extremely deformed bodies due to leprosy infection. The patients were from a slum area in Janakpur in the Terai. The area was known as Zero Mile because the leprosy-affected people living in slums were seen by others as 'nothing'. One lady was encouraged to stand up on her very badly eroded feet, close her eyes and to turn around like a ballerina. The joy on her face was electric. How privileged I felt!

Respect has been one of the major factors that has shaped my Nepal experience. I totally respect and admire most people in Nepal that I have met for their tenacity, practicality, dignity, and humility. I hope that that does not come over as patronising. I am truly in awe of them, and feel humbled, and sometimes ashamed, of my inadequacies, particularly in the practical departments. What the women can do with a standpipe or any running water to wash their clothes is incredible when I sometimes struggle with remembering which button to press on my automatic washer and dryer.

I am a strong believer in showing all people respect, especially if you want respect from others. I do try not to be rude or nasty to anyone unless, of course, they really deserve it and then I let rip. I have worked in shops and the service industry for many years and have learnt that it costs nothing to be polite and respectful, and in return you will usually get the best out of others. I can honestly say that, overall, when having direct contact with people, I have only ever been treated with respect.

That is not to say that I have not been laughed at, especially as I am somewhat larger than an average Nepali woman and have been in situations where I have been the only Western woman around. I recall that on one of my earlier visits two elderly men stood within a foot of me and were obviously talking about me at great length. They walked off when they had exhausted their conversation. At least they did not talk behind my back. I did not regard that behaviour as disrespectful but as cultural differences. People tend to be more open and less inhibited than in the West. On those occasions when I do not know what people are saying about me or are staring at me, I make up a conversation that they are discussing my incredible beauty or tasteful style. That usually works, although on my 'bad' days I can develop a complex.

I have been told bluntly that I am fat or old. This was more out of childish forwardness than being disrespectful. One man in Pokhara came running to me. We had met the previous year. He was so happy and said that I looked so much healthier than last year. I said, "Do you mean I look fatter than last year?". He said "Yes". I thanked him and told him that because we were in Nepal, I accepted his compliment, but if we had been in the UK, I would have slapped him across the face. "We do not comment on women's weight". We both laughed but I think he got the point.

I think that my age is a big factor in my 'cosy feeling' while I am in Nepal. Elderly people, in general, are treated respectfully by Nepali people. Their definition of elderly is a lot younger than our definition. I have been elderly since I was in my early fifties according to the Nepalese. Elderly people are given a higher status in Nepal than what I have found in the UK. They are treated with more respect and are bestowed with more wisdom. In general, the elderly are 'looked after' by their families. Lots of evidence, both academic and anecdotal, has shown that one reason why more traditional families will have many children is to ensure that they will be looked after in their old age. This was certainly true in the past. Some years ago, I befriended a Nepalese student at my university who returned to Nepal after only a few months. One reason was that she could not cope with our culture. She could not understand why so many elderly people were having to do their own shopping and carry heavy bags. It would never have happened in her family.

Terminology is an important factor with regards to respect towards others. 'Didi' is a familiar term given to a woman who is older than you and means 'older sister'. This is an address that has been used towards me for most of my visits in Nepal. I like this as I feel accepted by others. In more recent years I have been called 'ama', mother. This is being used more frequently since I stopped dying my hair and so am now *au naturelle*. I can cope with this most times, especially when I am missing my children. However, I do object to being called 'bajyai', grandmother. Fortunately, I have not been called this too much. It is not good for my morale.

Many people in Nepal want to leave their country to seek a better life in the UK, Australia, or USA. I totally get where they are coming from. Young people, particularly, see and speak to people from Western countries who have afforded the air fare to Nepal, and live a hugely different lifestyle because of earning more money. They see it as 'development' and financially it is. Indeed, over the years I have seen a lot of development in Nepal, but not always for the best. More transport does not necessarily mean a cleaner environment. Bulldozing family homes, albeit shanties, to make way for a pleasant shopping area or open recreational space does not help the homeless situation. But I feel sad when people want 'our' development. I try to tell them that with development comes a lot of negative consequences, most importantly, the breakdown of family and societal values which are the cornerstones of Nepali culture. Indeed, much of traditional society in Nepal is very much as I enjoyed as a child in the UK, with close extended families, leaving your door unlocked and being able to play safely outside; attributes that this generation are missing.

I undoubtedly found out my strengths and weaknesses. The many hours of sitting in waiting rooms and wards with Claire had taught me patience. Patience is something that needs to be mastered in Nepal as time management invariably is not a strong point for many Nepalese people. It is not unusual to arrange a meeting with someone who will arrive three hours late for no plausible reason. Or to go into a bank and come out after two hours of just sitting around. When I first went to Nepal, I had to put into practise my patience but to also learn to 'slow down'. It is a British trait to be obsessively punctual and most people become stressed out if that is not achieved. I had to adopt a more laid-back demeanour and plan to meet people at a more realistic '9 ish' or '3 ish', in other words, Nepali time.

A weakness that I found was my lack of tolerance in some situations. Because some things are simple in my eyes, I just expected it would be the same for other people. One instance was when I had made some six-piece jigsaws out of note paper with a drawing of a butterfly. I was astounded that the teachers at the nursery in Ghandruk where I was working could not fit them together. They were so easy to me. Another instance was when the teachers only washed the children's hands after they had eaten because they were visibly dirty. They could not see the need for them to wash their hands after going to the toilet or before eating as their hands looked clean and so couldn't be a threat.

These two incidents demonstrated the true meaning of ignorance. I do not mean this as a derogatory term of blaming the individuals as being stupid but as examples of a lack of awareness and knowledge. The teachers had never seen a jigsaw before so needed to get their head around the concept. They had only been taught literacy skills the year before and had not used educational toys as children. They had also not been aware of invisible germs. Would we have washed our hands before eating or after going to the toilet if we had not been taught to do it when we were children? I had to learn to accept and be more tolerant of other people's ignorance. I am pleased to say that the hygiene situation is much better now.

The trips did highlight to me that I had been brain washed over my lifetime with false perceptions of people and other cultures' ideals. I always thought that I was very open minded but when faced with some practices, such as, women marrying a tree, I realised that I had a very narrow mind towards non-scientific notions. When I first embarked on my PhD research, I interviewed many people asking about their beliefs of why people were infected with leprosy. The vast majority believed that it was because the sufferer had been wicked in their former life. As it was not scientific, I dismissed the belief as illogical. One evening I was talking to a Tibetan man who was very westernised in his dress and speech, so he must have the same beliefs as me. I told him of my findings and chuckled. He looked at me, straight in my eyes, and said, "Have you ever died?". "No" I said. "Well then how do you know it is not true?". Wow, that was a powerful moment. How could I be so arrogant, what right had I to belittle someone else's belief! That taught me such a valuable lesson. From that day I tried to be more open-minded, which not only helped me in my future research but, hopefully, to become a better person.

Seeing and meeting people who have gone through the most harrowing of experiences, has, hopefully, given me more empathy and compassion towards other people. How could you not be moved by tales of people watching their hands and feet erode in front of their eyes because of the consequences of leprosy, hearing a loved one being murdered by the Maoists, seeing their homes collapse during the earthquakes of 2015, taking in children from the street who had been sold into prostitution by their fathers for drink, caring for disabled children because their parents found it impossible to do so because of poverty or ignorance?

Many people ask me if it bothers me that I travel alone. Not at all. I can be totally selfish; I can do what I want, when I want and where I want. I don't have to consult anyone else. Saying that, the odd time I have had someone with me has also been good. Each person came with a different interest in mind, whether it be religion, geography or education which allowed me to 'revisit' Nepal through new eyes. However, it has been empowering to be a lone female traveller. I have met many independent women from numerous countries who have taken time out to volunteer or just travel around Nepal or even the World. It is such a joy to talk to and learn so much from them. It feels energising to be part of such an exciting collection of women, even if it is for a short time.

As a result of my time in Nepal my confidence has grown a million-fold. Just by having to travel on my own and to look after myself has boosted my independence and self-esteem. Having to bargain and to hold my own when confronted with difficulties has certainly made me more assertive, to the point of being stroppy sometimes, according to my husband. Pushing my boundaries, both physical and mental has made me less fearful of seizing new opportunities. My life has been so enriched by my jaunts in Nepal, beyond my wildest dreams. I have learnt so much about life and, particularly about myself, that I like to think that I have grown as a person. There is a popular phrase seen around Nepal, 'Don't try to change Nepal, let Nepal change you'. How true, for me anyway.

Printed in Great Britain
by Amazon